Gourmet Shops of Paris

an epicurean tour

Text by Pierre Rival
Photography by Christian Sarramon

Gourmet Shops of Paris

an epicurean tour

Flammarion

Contents

Paris offers more than a gastronomic feast, it is a city where taking a quiet stroll could lead you into culinary temptation. And such enticement extends beyond restaurants. In recent years, the city has seen the arrival of a series of small and often beautiful specialist food shops, bucking a trend in which local shops were losing out to their larger out-of-town rivals. And—as if the city needed to remind itself that it is still the capital of good food and drink—those shops that have been around forever have had a makeover.

CONFECTIONERY AND CHOCOLATES
Heaven on earth: the displays at La Mère de Famille and Legrand, the marshmallows at L'Étoile d'Or, and the chocolates at Jean Paul Hévin and the Maison du Chocolat, and particularly ambrosiac at Pierre Marcolini, a Belgian chocolate maker now based in Paris.

CAKES, LARGE AND SMALL
Including Ladurée macaroons, cakes from Bertrand, green-tea cakes from Patisserie Sadaharu Aoki, and Algerian pastries from La Bague de Kenza.

TEA AND COFFEE
Take in the mysterious surroundings and refined interior of the Maison des Trois Thés and the joys of the tearooms and boutiques at Mariage Frères. Stop by one of the many Richard stores or the famous Verlet near Palais Royal.

BREAD AND CHEESE
Bread, in all its forms, from Kayser, the *Moulin de la Vierge*, Poilâne, and Paul. Season by season the cheese maker's art is revealed at Barthélémy and Anne Marie Cantin.

FINE FOOD STORES
Fabulous olive oils from around the world at Oliviers & Co., Alicante, and J. Leblanc. Spanish hams from Bellota Bellota and Da Rosa, salmon and caviar from Petrossian, and truffles from Terre de Truffes. Spices from Izrael and French regional products from the Pipalottes Gourmandes and the Comptoir de la Gastronomie.

P.120
Paris in a glass

FAMOUS AND LESSER-
KNOWN WINE MERCHANTS
Paris has an enduring love affair
with wine, from classic *grands
crus* to the biodynamic brews
of the new growers. Lavinia—
unique in Europe—is the first
department store for wine.
Les Caves Augé stocks the
finest of fine wines. At La
Dernière Goutte Parisians can
discover regional wines thanks
to the efforts of an American
in Paris. De Vinis Illustribus
caters to collectors. Legrand
organizes tasting sessions
for both connoisseurs and
beginners alike.

P.138
Paris on the go

SMALL SNACKS
There may be a worldwide mania
for snacking, but Parisians are
the world's most demanding
snackers: homemade soups
at the Bar à Soupes and Soupe
et Quenelles, delicious Italian
charcuterie at La Crémerie,
sandwiches and wraps at Cojean,
not to mention the baroque
creations at the Bon Marché's
Delicabar, and at Pomze apples in
every form at Pomze, the first
boutique devoted to the fruit and
its innumerable possibilities.

P.161
The gourmet's notebook

The authors have made
a selection of the best
of gourmet Paris that will
satisfy the most discerning
gourmands; but the reader
is bound to complete it with
his or her own discoveries,
because when it comes to
the subject of food, Paris's
appetite is inexhaustible.

Paris—a gourmet's paradise. The number of first-class restaurants, bistros, and brasseries and the standards they maintain is evidence of this incontestable fact. But it is a pity to reduce the city's gastronomic pleasures to this aspect alone, and in doing so to neglect many of the other very real pleasures to be had from a stroll through the city. A trip to any local patisserie or bakery, or a rummage through the bric-a-brac of a grocery store will give you an idea of the temptations Parisians are faced with every day, and such constant exposure has a tendency to turn every promenade into an aperitif. In this book we have put together an itinerary for those interested in discovering the city's culinary curiosities. To facilitate that journey we have assembled a selection of the finest—and most beautiful—boutiques the city has to offer, the ones where all thoughts of diets and good resolutions are reduced to nothing.

The French capital is undergoing a number of culinary revolutions. The emergence of a "Paris School" of chocolate is one of them, a renaissance in patisserie is another. In all corners of the city one hears increasingly about the "French art of tea," as if this was something that had existed forever, and experts now come from the Orient to Paris in order to promote their finest teas. In the 1920s, Paris "invented" caviar from sturgeon roe. At the dawn of the twenty-first century the city that soaks up culinary fashions like a sponge has gone crazy for Spanish cured ham and promotes it the world over as if it had been invented there. The same is true for olive oil, which Paris has helped to rejuvenate as a commodity and whose cardiovascular benefits it has trumpeted, far from its Mediterranean origins. Even in wine—a domain in which Paris's leading role has long since been ceded to London—a host of new wine merchants, keen to shake free of the dictates of the traditional labels of old, have shown their ingenuity and initiative by promoting "organic" wines, destined to become the *grands crus* of tomorrow. Parisians have also become adept consumers of snacks and sandwiches, thanks to a lightness and freshness that is new to these traditionally Anglo-Saxon specialties. And the choice of bread in the city, once limited to the humble baguette, has multiplied beyond belief.

Paris is now a gastronomic party open to all comers. Never has there been such attention to quality, originality, and unadulterated gastronomic pleasure in the city as at present. At a time when the future of small neighborhood shops looks increasingly perilous, this can only be a good thing. Because as new shops open around the city—whether in its chic arrondissements or bohemian quarters—those devoted to gastronomy seem to succeed and prosper best. Proof, if it were needed, that despite Paris's reputation for fickleness, when it comes to one of civilization's fundamental pillars—culinary pleasure—it knows how to steer a clear course.

The windows at Paul (preceding page) and
Le Comptoir de la Gastronomie (facing page) demonstrate
the dynamism of Paris's food-and-beverage sector:
in constant search of new ideas, it nevertheless remains
faithful to time-honored traditions and values.

Sweet
Paris

Confectionery and chocolates

Some people might consider Paris's claim to be one of the world's chocolate capitals just a little presumptuous. After all, Spain maintains that it was the first to introduce chocolate to Europe, and England that it was the first to eat solid chocolate—in a famous incarnation known as the "Spanish pudding." Honors also go to Switzerland for inventing the technique that gave us bars of chocolate, to Holland for cocoa powder, to Austria for the Sacher torte, to Italy for chocolate truffles, and again to Switzerland for milk chocolate. We owe the mass production of chocolate bars to the United States, and are indebted to Belgium for coming up with the first solid chocolate shells that are now used as receptacles for praline, toffee, or cream. Although France was already host to many chocolate aficionados in the sixteenth century, it cannot be said that French confectioners played a pivotal role in the slow evolution of the delicacy that has since become indispensable to our palates. Nevertheless, in the twenty-first century, the eyes of the world's chocolate lovers are increasingly turning to Paris. This is not because the city's confectioners have come up with some new method of processing the cocoa bean. It is due to the way they have refined traditional presentation to the point that, in Paris, chocolate has gone beyond its original role as a mere delicacy to become a gastronomic food in its own right. And what was once relegated to the fields of craftsmanship or industry has since been raised to the level of art. Parisian chocolate makers, or those who have set up in Paris, cannot be content simply to reproduce recipes from the repertory that have proved their worth in the past. Faced with an educated and demanding public that is quick to compare chocolate not with goods from other chocolate makers but rather with the very best that Paris's rich gastronomic landscape has to offer, chocolate makers need constantly to refine their art to make their mark. In the land of the "must-have," the chocolate maker is expected to surpass himself in his quest to attain the summit of refinement.

JEAN-PAUL HÉVIN

It is not just the boutiques that have a design edge at Jean-Paul Hévin. For the round chocolate lollipops enclosed in a square wrapping and made from 70 percent cocoa, the details of the packaging are vital.

Jean-Paul Hévin embodies this ambition. Honored with the title of *Meilleur Ouvrier de France* for his pastry in 1986, he first worked with Joël Robuchon at the Hôtel Nikko before running the Peltier chocolate store in Tokyo and then opening his first store in Paris on avenue de la Motte-Picquet. Hévin calls himself a "chocolate artist" and his creations "signature chocolates" in direct reference to the "signatures" found on haute couture labels. What is so special about his "signature"? First, there is the attention he pays to the quality of his raw materials. "I never delegate the task of tasting to anyone," he says, and his exceptional palate can detect what he calls the "different levels of taste" in the various cocoa beans he uses, mainly from Venezuela, Ecuador, Colombia, and Madagascar. As a chocolate maker, Hévin is primarily a first-class taster of chocolate whose aim is not to alter the flavors he detects, but to enhance them through combinations that are both surprising and delicious. This has led him to invent so-called "dynamic chocolates" filled with preserved ginger and mixed with spices like cola nuts and *bois bandé*, and "chocolate-cheese aperitifs" flavored with cheeses, such as Époisses, Pont l'Évêque, goat cheese, and Roquefort, and best savored with a *vin jaune* from the Jura region. But Hévin's style can also be seen in his approach to the classics. The finesse of a plain ganache filling comes from the perfect proportion of cocoa; a spiced version uses cinnamon, ginger, coffee, or honey; fruit flavors incorporate lime, grape, orange, raspberry, or blackcurrant; praline variations use the best hazelnuts, almonds, or nougatine; and the milk chocolates come in plain, caramel, truffle, and gianduja varieties. All burst with heady aromas, while the fine chocolate that surrounds them melts on the tongue before revealing the subtle flavors contained within.

"Chocolate is like wine," says Hévin. "From a single ingredient you can make a wide variety of products, and without variety there is no pleasure." What is his definition of pleasure? "I want to make chocolates that are full of flavor and fresh tasting, which generate well-being, tenderness, and even poetry in those who taste them. In short, I want to provide a moment of happiness." Happiness through chocolate—now there is something that Parisian chocolate makers can be proud to claim as their contribution to the history of the cocoa bean.

Pierre Marcolini is Parisian by adoption but Belgian by birth. Already well known both in his native land and internationally, he came to Paris looking for further recognition and respect. And he deserves it, because he is one of the few remaining European chocolate makers who still make their own *couverture*. To the uninitiated this may not seem radical, but it is a genuine declaration of

MARCOLINI

In his rue Bonaparte boutique, Pierre Marcolini exhibits his chocolates the way a museum would its greatest treasures. His obsession with the fine coating of his chocolates makes these square and heart-shaped creations utterly irresistible.

independence, because Marcolini makes his own chocolate from raw cocoa beans—like nineteenth-century confectioners did—and he wants everyone to know. And for that Paris, world capital of all things gastronomic, is the best place to be. "Making chocolate from scratch means you get to know your material better," he explains. "Making it yourself also means you use only what you know to be the very best ingredients." His vanilla comes from Tahiti, and he incorporates violets or cinnamon at the early stages of the process instead of adding extracts at the end as a shortcut. Having chosen to manufacture his own chocolate has changed the way he exercises his chosen profession in other ways, too. Marcolini spends a significant part of each year visiting cocoa-producing regions so that he can choose his own beans. This has resulted in personal relationships with certain growers, large shares of whose crops he purchases—at fair trade prices, of course. That is how, for the last few years, he has bought the entire crop produced by a Mexican grower, Clara Echevaria, who has been fighting to save her exceptional variety of 100 percent *criollo* cocoa bean, the *porcelana*, with its aromas of rose and jasmine. And Parisians, ever conscious of the importance of the region of production, can now buy the first bar of chocolate made entirely from the *porcelana* bean, which Marcolini calls the "Carré Chocolat—Limited Edition." Given its extraordinary "mouth feel," and magnificent aroma, tasting it is akin to drinking the finest of wines.

In order to make his own *couverture*, Marcolini had to find both the machines and the techniques that were used in the past and had been forgotten due to industrialization. He gave the machines he managed to find in flea markets across Europe to retired Belgian confectioners, who were the only ones left who knew how to use them. From them he learned how to crush the bean, remove the skin, and transform it into a smooth paste, which is then kneaded with sugar and vanilla. He brought back the old technique of heating the paste to release the good lactic acids, while simultaneously driving off the bad ones. In short, he took control of the cocoa's fermentation process. By making his own *couverture*, Marcolini is also free to flavor it as he wishes by introducing coffee, cardamom, or ginger at the roasting stage. But whether they are round or square, all of Pierre Marcolini's chocolates are remarkable for their crunchiness due to the thickness of the chocolate casing that makes up at least 40 percent of the total weight of each chocolate. This detracts in no way from their subtlety or finesse, but instead gives them a distinct personality, and one that is bound to seduce those ardent cocoa lovers who recognize chocolate for what it really is—a genuine luxury item that is really quite rare.

MARCOLINI

Pierre Marcolini's boutique, designed by Yan Pennor, one of the rising stars of French design, with its exotic woods and immaculate window displays is the chocolate equivalent of a jewelry box.

Paris is also the capital of French chocolate made by smaller regional confectioners, of which there are many. Just beside the Moulin Rouge is the L'Étoile d'Or, run by Denise Acabo, an obligatory stop for all those who—unlike Acabo—don't have the time to visit the many excellent chocolate makers outside Paris. With her braids and tartan dresses, some might consider Acabo eccentric, but if she is, it is in a way that makes her passionate about her subject and impervious to fashions or the passage of time. What is her specialty? Chocolate, of course, but also confectionery in general. Her little boutique welcomes the foreign tourists who seem to come straight from the buses that deposit them on boulevard Rochechouart. They come for Acabo, her impeccable palate, and her forthright views. For those chocolate makers who don't have a store of their own in Paris, to be selected by Acabo is equivalent to a national badge of honor. Mind you, she will only accept the very best and even from them she chooses their best items—the crème de la crème—for her boutique.

A visit to Acabo's boutique is like a crash course in the best that French chocolate making has to offer. Start with the world-famous chocolate master from the Rhone valley, Maurice Bernachon. The son Jean-Jacques upholds the family tradition by making his own *couverture* and roasting beans that come from only the finest sources: Puerto Cabello, Guayaquil, Santa Fe, San Antonio, Madagascar, Jamaica, and Bahia. In the finest tradition, these are combined with the best ingredients—butter from Échiré, cream from Isigny, and the choicest vanilla pods—to produce truly luxurious chocolates that are renowned for their richness and finesse. A visit to the shop is proof of Bernachon's international success with visitors from as far as Tokyo and New York. Denise Acabo carries the full range of Bernachon chocolate in Paris, and is the only boutique to do so. Particularly noteworthy is Bernachon's Palet d'Or, made from *crème fraîche*, dark chocolate, and decorated with gold leaf, and Aveline, with praline made from genuine Piedmont hazelnuts and wrapped in the finest chocolate. Don't miss his extraordinary range of chocolate bars, particularly the fruit-and-nut and nougatine varieties.

The goods of other French regional chocolate makers are on display in the delightfully old-fashioned shelves and windows of L'Étoile d'Or: look out for Bernard Dufoux from La Clayette in Burgundy. His dark chocolate with figs and prunes, and the aphrodisiac mini-log filled with ginger are especially noteworthy. Delicia—little more than a gram of pure cocoa each—are made by Palomas in Lyon, as are Fourvières, small, cocoa-wrapped pralines covered in coffee-flavored meringue. Stéphane Bonnat from Voiron is represented by the Krugette, a strip of candied orange peel dipped in chocolate fondant, and the Sicilian, a honey and rum fondant encased in chocolate

L'ÉTOILE D'OR
Just a stone's throw from Pigalle is the nearest thing there is to a living museum of French confectionery. And make no mistake, Denise Acabo has personally tasted and selected all of the specialties she has on display. Facing page: Marshmallows and a vintage box of Nancy macaroons. Below: Hard candy, caramels, and bonbons.

L'ÉTOILE D'OR

*A tiny boutique packed
with boxes and jars,
dominated by a large window
display full of chocolates.
L'Étoile d'Or is like
a chocolate antique
dealer where you come
to hunt down some
forgotten treasure.*

À LA MÈRE DE FAMILLE

*À la Mère de Famille on
rue du Faubourg Montmartre
has been for many years the
place where well-behaved
children come to be rewarded.
Above: Hard candy, frimousse
lollipops and mouth-watering
fruit candies.
Following pages: Display
cases, which have remained
unchanged since the nineteenth
century, filled with treasures,
and crystalized rose petals—
the sight alone delights old
and young alike.*

fondant. Acabo selects each item with one key stipulation: she must have the exclusive distribution rights in Paris because, as she says, "I am very selective, and I want to be the only one to stock them." And she doesn't confine herself to chocolate. Her boutique is like a merry-go-round where each ride ends with a treat, the stuff of children's dreams. From the Basque country in southwestern France come the black cherries produced by Goizetik; from Corsica, organic jams and chestnut purée made by Marie-Claude Scarbonichi; Fouque's nougat from Signes in Provence is guaranteed to be 100 percent honey and almonds; the toffees from Quiberon are from Henri Le Roux. Acabo has them all there, unexpected delights that are the best in French confectionery. One might have thought this world lost, were it not for Denise Acabo's insistence that it is not and her Noah's ark of a boutique that proves it.

À la Mère de Famille is yet another treasure trove that looks like something out of a short story by Guy de Maupassant. The store's name is appropriate since elegant mothers still congregate here—with or without their offspring. The window is always beautifully decorated for the main holidays, particularly Easter when the eggs are exuberantly decorated. The boutique owns a workshop in Saint-Avertin, outside Tours, where it makes its own chocolate, and sells a chocolate cake kit that includes the necessary dark chocolate and ground almonds—as well as the recipe, of course. À la Mère de Famille specialties include plain ganaches flavored with alcohol, puff pastries that melt in the mouth, and the Mokaresse, a walnut kernel wrapped in a coffee-flavored ganache set on a slice of nougatine. Customers seem to come to À la Mère de Famille first and foremost to treat themselves, beginning with a feast for the eyes. The boutique's "interior" looks the same as it did in the late nineteenth century, when it first opened. The same jars are still used to store the candied fruits, angelica, orange and lemon peel, and glace cherries that decorate the cakes, and

LA MAISON DU CHOCOLAT

Between Étoile and Monceau park lies a culinary temple, the chocolate equivalent of haute couture. Facing page: Close-up of the seductively shaped rum-flavored chocolate truffle mousse bouchée.

the same windows display the multiple pastel shades of the mouthwatering almond delicacies—*calissons* and *amandins* flavored with orange vodka, prunes in Armagnac, and walnuts in kirsch—as well as tempting *grignotines*, or nibbles, made from chocolate and orange. The fruit jellies are handmade in the Auvergne region, the candied chestnuts come from the Ardèche region—as they should—the multicolored hard candies come in flavors such as violet-poppy and caramel, and the pralines come from Montargis in central France. The cash register, in copper and wood, is taller than a confessional; the assistants still serve as in times past, dressed in white aprons and gloves; and as you leave, they might suggest you buy a "little face" lollipop. Try as one might, it is impossible to resist the old-fashioned charm of À la Mère de Famille, a charm that is guaranteed to send you back to your childhood.

"You are a wizard with ganache," said Jean-Paul Aron, philosopher and author of *Le Mangeur du XIXe siècle,* of Robert Linxe. It was in 1987, and Linxe had just opened his second Maison du Chocolat in Paris on rue François 1er. Since then, three more have opened in Paris, making a total of five; there are two each in London and Tokyo, and one in New York. Furthermore, La Maison du Chocolat has joined the Comité Colbert, the exclusive reserve of France's leading luxury goods firms. While chocolate may have brought Linxe a long way from his Basque origins, it is worth remembering just how audacious he was in being the first to open a store devoted entirely to chocolate. But then again his chocolates, which he has been selling since 1977, were not like any chocolates available then. He set out to reinvent chocolate and knew exactly how to go about it: by creating an aesthetic emotion around it. He knew that he wanted the experience of tasting each mouthful of chocolate to be comparable to that of tasting a wonderful dish or of contemplating a great work of art, and that to achieve this he would need to attain "excellence, savoir-faire, and good taste." These became his watchwords and governed his whole approach. Excellent ingredients: Robert Linxe ensured that only the very finest chocolate from Valrhona—maker of the best chocolate for use by patissiers—made its way into his products and closely followed the development of the cocoa used. Technical perfection: he learned this during his career as a caterer and by ensuring that the best pastry chefs in the business came to work for him, starting with Pascal Le Gac who is now responsible for the creative side of the business. Good taste: Linxe's good taste was confirmed by the rapturous reception that Paris's gourmets gave to the characteristics of his chocolate—a casing that is super-fine, crunchy, and, above all, neutral so as

to highlight the flavors of each ganache; associating different types of chocolate to achieve the perfect balance between the responses of the various senses and the flavors of the filling; and the variety of innovative flavorings that never distract from the taste of the chocolate. Take, for example, the Andalousie, one of La Maison du Chocolat's most popular creations. Inside a casing that is lower in cocoa content so as not to interfere with the taste and texture of the filling, a delicate assembly of strong chocolate from Trinidad, offset by a milder one from Ghana, gives way to a zing of lemon zest that has been lightly infused in cream. The result is both delicious and eminently satisfying. In the Zagora, on the other hand, the strength of the fresh mint infusion is heightened by the chocolate from Trinidad, and the outcome is distinctly refreshing. For the Garrigue, Robert Linxe has combined a small proportion of flowery Madagascar chocolate with a much more assertive chocolate from Ecuador. This combination enhances the flavor of a fennel infusion which is in turn accentuated with a little star aniseed that underlines the unexpected licorice taste. In each of these chocolates, as in everything that La Maison du Chocolat does, the hallmarks are a light filling, and clear and precise aromas. Truly, these are chocolates to make your mouth water.

LA MAISON DU CHOCOLAT
At the Maison du Chocolat pleasure comes with every new flavor, each guaranteed to produce new emotions. Facing page: Baskets of praline chocolates. Above from left to right: Prunes with chocolate, chocolate, caramel éclairs, and the mousse of marrons glacés in dark or milk chocolate.

Cakes, large and small

Although the cake may come at the end of the meal, the true Parisian gourmet always leaves room for desert. The habit goes back to childhood. On Sundays, only the sight of cakes on the family dining table was consolation for an otherwise interminably dull day. Any Parisian worth his salt will regale you with stories about his neighborhood patisserie, but is still capable of going from one end of the city to the other (and beyond if necessary) to taste an *opéra* here, a *mille-feuille* there, or a baba just about anywhere.

For a long time, tearooms were simply an excuse for indulging in cakes and pastries under the pretext that one was just having tea with one's friends. And for a long time, the patisserie was an appendage to the bakery where, while choosing a baguette or *pain de campagne*, one could commit the venal sin of looking in the window where the *vacherins* and charlottes lay dormant, and on special occasions—at Christmas, or for a birthday—yield to temptation and splurge. Sunday was the day when cakes were always permitted. Sunday in Paris was dull beyond belief and only distinguished from fast days by the brightly colored ribbons that wrapped the inevitable cake box that lit up the eyes of expectant children.

Today's Parisian fully owns up to his liking for sweet things by selecting a few choice places that are not ashamed of being temples to cake. He goes there regularly, at any time of the year and without

**PÂTISSERIE
SADAHARU AOKI**

*In deference to
his Japanese roots,
Sahaharu Aoki flavors his
macaroons and* financiers
with macha *green tea.*

PÂTISSERIE
SADAHARU AOKI

*Behind the minimalist façade
of his boutique on rue de
Vaugirard lie Sadaharu Aoki's
exotically flavored creations.
But Aoki is classically
trained, and his millefeuilles,
éclairs, chocolate croissants,
and Danish pastries adhere
to the strictest traditions of the
French pastry chef's art.*

feeling the need to justify himself. Cake has become an obsession, and in truth only attention to his figure and diet prevent him going to the patisserie more often. And even that is changing. Because those clever patissiers have reduced the amount of sugar, flour, and eggs they use to the strict minimum. In order to seduce their clients, the thick, heavy creams of the past have been replaced by smooth, airy mousses; the choux and puff pastries are made ever lighter; and the range of fillings—in ever increasing varieties—change every season, much like the collections of fashion designers. So the once humble patisserie has become a boutique, as fashionable and elegant as a fashion store, where the environment—fun and gourmet at the same time—sets out to feed the eye in preparation for the gastronomic feast to come. Even their interiors borrow heavily from that of fashion. Be it the strict formalism of Sadaharu Aoki or the kitsch interior of Les Cakes de Bertrand there is something for all tastes. It is as if today's pastry chefs, with a nod to the great nineteenth-century chef Antonin Carême's statement that pastry is "the principal branch of architecture," see themselves as interior designers as much as purveyors of gourmet pleasure—perhaps to compensate for what cakes have lost in scale and grandeur since Carême's time.

Sadaharu Aoki has done things his way. The Japanese pastry chef has quickly become a part of Paris's culinary landscape thanks to his training by a series of master chefs. After having initially apprenticed in the legendary Lucien Peltier patisserie on rue de Sèvres (ironically, a branch now exists in Tokyo), Aoki went on to work at La Méditerranée restaurant on place de l'Odéon before taking up a post with Freddy Girardet at his Michelin three-star restaurant in Crissier, outside Lausanne. Aoki returned to Paris to work at one of the bastions of traditional pastry, Couderc on boulevard Voltaire. During his training, his hard work was rewarded with a string of prizes: finalist in the Mandarin Napoléon competition, second place in the Charles Proust prize three times, Peltier

LES CAKES DE BERTRAND
You could be forgiven if you first go to Les Cakes de Bertrand, situated in the Nouvelle Athènes area of Paris, for its kitsch elegance, but you are sure to return for the quality of what is on offer, such as the boxes of chocolates and cherry pastries (following pages).

Trophy in Arpajon, and winner of the Jean-Louis Berthelot Trophy in Romorantin. With such an exemplary track record, the Japanese apprentice can now proudly call himself a great French patissier. When Aoki decided to open his own boutique at the end of 2001, he had a clear idea of what he wanted, based on his intimate knowledge of Western and Eastern culture. "In Paris, there are plenty of good pastry chefs, but not as many beautiful patisseries; whereas in Japan, the reverse is true," he said in an interview with the trade paper *Le Journal du Pâtissier*. He aimed to create a synthesis of the two approaches.

When you step inside his store on rue de Vaugirard, you are struck by the clinical sterility of the place and the almost glacial interior, which might be off-putting were it not for the cakes, perfectly lined up in the window like so many sparkling jewels. And at this level of perfection, the nearest comparison is indeed jewelry. Aoki has brought traditional pastry to the highest level possible in a way that only a pupil who has gone beyond the level of his teachers can do. What strikes one most at a tasting is not so much the exotically flavored pastry creams (including green tea) that he uses to fill his *mille-feuilles* and éclairs; rather, it is the near perfection of the cakes themselves. "I always use the best ingredients," he points out, whether it is butter from the Charente region, wheat flour for choux pastry, seasonal fruits for his fillings, or the eggs and ground almonds that go into his sponges. Everything else comes down to impeccable technique. The base of his éclair, for example, is as round and crusty as a baguette. To achieve this effect, Aoki uses three baking trays instead of the usual one and bakes the éclairs in a moderately hot oven—300°F (150°C)—for thirty or forty minutes instead of the usual fifteen to twenty minutes. As a result, the pastry base doesn't go soggy when the filling is introduced, and produces a delicious contrast of textures. Like the chefs who spend their energies on reworking one recipe with maniacal attention to detail until they achieve perfect harmony rather than inventing something new, Aoki can have a limited selection of cakes on offer. This Japanese-Parisian chef is a worthy representative of the best in traditional craftsmanship. While you may first be drawn into his boutique by the steel-and-glass Bauhaus-style window, you will come back for his unforgettable cakes that are like so many intangible reminders of the greatness of French patisserie.

Move on to Les Cakes de Bertrand, a miniscule store on rue Bourdaloue. The curtains, festooned with frills and flounces, give the impression that it has been here since time immemorial, or at least since the time that the first Romantics made what was then a far-flung suburb of Paris

their new Athens in the 1820s. But take a closer look inside the tearoom that appears so old. The humor begins to stand out. True, there are plenty of gilded, baroque frames around, but look closer at what's in them and you have to admit that the paintings are anything but innocent scenes of country life. They are wonderfully offbeat reminders of happy times in the last century—the 1920s, the 1960s—when "Paris was a party." A miniature Ritz, like one carved on a grain of rice, which, if it were meant to be serious would be pompous, but instead is subtly ironic. And what is there to eat at Bertrand's place? What can someone whom we know to be so crafty as to mask his true intentions when it comes to decorating offer us in the sugar line? What sort of pastries can be created by someone with such postmodernist sensibilities? Cakes, of course, but then we discover that grandmother's cake comes in both sweet and savory varieties, in fruit and spice versions. Didier Bertrand—his full name—is not a professional pastry chef, which is perhaps why he has been able to take such liberties with the traditional classic recipes he first tasted as a child. This dietician, who "sold out to the enemy," as he likes to say, has a motto hanging above his cash register that states, "No gourmand can be happy." And so he busies himself with our happiness with the fervor of the self-taught and knows no limits. Next to the traditional fruitcakes he proposes a range of sponge cakes flavored with chocolate, spices, natural flavorings, and flowers. He has taken the cake out of its sugary ghetto and reincarnated it in a variety of savory guises. To achieve this, he needed to perfect a softer cake mix, to which he added a little grated cheese. And thus began his transformation of the humble cake: cake with fourme d'Ambert, a blue cheese from the Auvergne; cakes with olives, bacon, and fennel seeds; cakes with tandoori chicken. At last, the cake had found its savior. Like many contemporary artists, Bernard enjoys taking a theme and exploring all the possible variations on that theme. Put simply, he likes constantly to recreate his ideas. The familiar

LES CAKES DE BERTRAND
Les Cakes de Bertrand,
a miniature gastronomic temple,
has a fine selection of teas,
jams, and chocolate cakes.

cake lends itself well to this treatment. Ingenious gourmet Bertrand had already applied the same recipe to another staple: soup. In his first boutique, behind the Gare Saint-Lazare, he concocted crazy varieties of soup like "Tibetan" bouillon with pearl barley, ginger, and fresh goat's cheese; chilled cream of zucchini; and tomato soup with Moroccan spices. What runs through all of these ideas and draws them together is the notion of a range, a series, a collection, much like those of fashion designers. It is no surprise that the Les Cakes de Bertrand name now appears on a line of fashion accessories. The link with fashion was implicitly present in the boutique's offbeat décor from the outset. All that was missing was the opportunity to cement that link.

LA BAGUE DE KENZA

*Mounds of oriental cakes
at La Bague de Kenza in the
République neighborhood will
tempt you on first sight. Lose
yourself in the atmosphere here
as you enjoy the authentic
Algerian specialties that are
lighter and slightly less sweet,
to suit French tastes.
Following pages: Djiriates—
traditional Algerian cakes made
from almonds, honey, and
vanilla, and marzipan pears
that are all the better when
served with a mint tea.*

That opportunity came with Bernard Castelain—a chocolate maker from Chateauneuf du Pape—and his trendily wrapped chocolate bars. "We couldn't just let our customers stick these precious items into any old bag. They deserved a casket, something made to measure," says Bertrand, by way of explanation of how his famous "chocolate pouches," exactly the size of a bar, came to be made. The pouches, varying in style from glamorous to romantic, were a surprise hit, and are now sold in four hundred outlets around the world. "For the gourmet, they fulfill a dual function: that of protecting the precious bar and that of slowly revealing the object of desire." Les Cakes de Bertrand has further strengthened the links between fashion and food. There is also a range of shopping bags and change purses. Bertrand has resolutely refused to set up a catering activity, though he makes an exception when it comes to catering for backstage parties at the fashion shows of designers like Yohji Yamamoto and Yves Saint Laurent. In doing so, he is affirming the strong links that exist between the worlds of high fashion and gastronomy.

Samira Fahim likes to be precise: her patisserie has its origins in Algiers. Five years ago, the dynamic Fahim opened a boutique on rue Saint-Maur to the delight of the "bourgeois bohemians" who populate the rue Oberkampf neighborhood. Behind the store windows, pyramids of golden cakes are piled high, catching the eye and making the mouth water. In this store straight out of *The Thousand and One Nights*, everything is abundant: towers of baklava, mountains of *makrouts*, and swathes of *cornes de gazelles* fill the space. But Fahim sticks to her guns, admitting that her pastries have Turkish origins from the time that Algiers was ruled by a bey. So while the walnut baklava may come from Constantine, she prefers the almond version from Algiers, although both are available. And that is La Bague de Kenza's secret. It sees itself as a little outpost of Bab-el-Oued in Paris, which guarantees its authenticity. Everything else is just a question of taste, and Fahim is generous enough to offer

specialties from the other regions of Algeria. What is striking about her pastries—all fairly traditional—is their lightness. The lightness that is found in pastry made using a minimum of shortening—margarine or sunflower oil—and in the hand that sprinkles the sugar or pours the honey. It makes you want to come back all the more often. When she crossed the Mediterranean, Fahim knew how to adapt delicious traditional Algerian pastries to European tastes, without for a moment sacrificing the intensity of flavor and aromas that characterize them. The result is a patisserie that is at the same time typically Algerian and firmly Parisian. La Bague de Kenza is now an established part of Paris's gourmet landscape and has not lost anything of its authentic roots.

Ladurée transcends fashion. It has been on the same site on rue Royale since 1862, and Paris's gourmets could probably make their way there blindfolded. One word explains all this: macaroons. Perfected in the early twentieth century by Pierre Desfontaines, the grandson of the founder Ernest Ladurée, this little petit four, by turns moist and dry—two shells made of roughly ground almonds, icing sugar, and egg white held together by a flavorsome ganache—should really be called a Ladurée in memory of its inventor, in the same way as the *madeleine* and the *tarte Tatin*. But there is no such thing as copyrighting a discovery in the world of pastry. Pierre Desfontaine's invention was to enrich a dry cake brought to France by Maria Medici and her Italian cooks, making it what the Americans call a "double-decker" and filling it with a delicious almond paste. It was a stroke of genius that transformed a simple "cookie" into a miniature delicacy as seductive as a Tanagra figurine. Because in a macaroon, everything contributes to the pleasure, starting with the curvaceous shape, both reassuring and tempting. Next, the color, originally subtle, has since taken on every hue of the spectrum in accordance with the flavors concocted by Ladurée's successors. And above all, its size, small, discreet, and yet so appetizing—without a moment's hesitation in one mouthful it is gone—make it an innocent pleasure par excellence. Such is the secret of the macaroon's success, and the formula hasn't changed in over a century.

Since 1997, Philippe Andrieu has reigned over the destiny of the Ladurée macaroon. This master pastry chef has a track record second to none: he worked with Georges Blanc at Vonnas and Michel Bras at Laguiole before arriving in Paris at the celebrated gourmet food store Fauchon. In the meantime, Ladurée opened a second branch on the Champs-Elysées and a third on rue Bonaparte in the sixth arrondissement to cater to those diehards who couldn't live without their daily dose of macaroons. And under Andrieu, the macaroon has mutated, with summer and winter collections and ever more fanciful, subtle, exotic, and surprising flavors: licorice, Amaretto-soaked cherry, basil and lime, aniseed, mint, Yunnan tea, and salted butter caramel. It was with the turn of the century that the house of Ladurée decided to treat itself to a new look, in the same way as great classics—a Chanel suit or a Vuitton bag—get a facelift from time to time. As a result, the eyes of a whole new generation turned to Ladurée, drawn by its macaroons. While traditionalists will be pleased to know that their old favorites—vanilla, coffee, and chocolate—are still available, colors as diverse as black, pink, and green are now also on offer and retain the essence of what macaroons are all about. Alongside this armada of macaroons, Andrieu produces a full range of delicacies,

LADURÉE

Ladurée on rue Jacob is the famous pastry shop that invented the macaroon. Whether for a business breakfast or a romantic afternoon snack, any excuse will do to enjoy a visit to this calmly luxurious tearoom. They also sell beautifully packaged gift boxes of fruit jellies, violet-flavored marshmallow, or fine chocolates.

LADURÉE

*Macaroons here come
in all flavors and colors
and change with the seasons.
In the window of the delightful
boutique, on the corner of rue
Jacob and rue Bonaparte,
macaroons are displayed
on cubes.*

each more tantalizing than the next, which follow Ladurée's formula: take a classic that has proven itself over time, and reinvent it. For summer, the Religieuse is coated in violet-flavored blackcurrant, rose-flavored raspberry, or cherry-pistachio. The Saint-Honoré, traditionally filled with vanilla pastry cream, receives a violet-blackcurrant or cherry-pistachio treatment, though its classic crown of whipped cream remains untouched. And of course there are today's inventions, the ones that may or may not stand the test of time. For Valentine's Day, Andrieu concocted a sponge in the shape of a four-leaved clover, each leaf of which was filled with an enticingly different combination: blackcurrant-violet, rose-raspberry, strawberry-poppy, and chocolate-mint. A mirror image of the modern and daring couples who go to Ladurée these days. And to satisfy those diehards who absolutely have to have their chocolate cake, he neutralizes the traditional sweetness by marrying chocolate cream with Sarawak pepper and lime zest, and coating it in a Java chocolate icing that highlights the bitterness and acidity so much in vogue these days among serious chocolate lovers. "What is important," he tells us, "is to give pleasure to our customers." And in doing this he is in keeping with the tradition of Ladurée, which built its reputation on always being perfectly in tune with the desires of Paris's most demanding food lovers.

We have mentioned Antonin Carême, who once famously said: "There are five branches of fine art: painting, sculpture, poetry, music, and architecture, whose principal branch is patisserie." This deserves to be taken more seriously than it usually is, because in France patisserie is taken very seriously indeed and the "Paris School," as we have seen throughout this chapter, has brought a distinctly French touch to this art form, namely classicism and balance coupled with finesse and attention to detail.

8362

THÉ
LOTUS
Blanc

MARIAGE 1854 FRÈRES

144

THÉ
NEIGE
DE JADE

MARIAGE 1854 FRÈRES

TIBET
Thé des

MARIAGE FRÈR

TIBET
Thé des Pri

MARIAGE FR

Tea and coffee

For the Chinese, Japanese, English, Russians, and Arabs, tea has always been a national drink. But what about the French? The French—or rather the Parisian—*salon de thé*, or tearoom, is a bit of a misnomer. In reality it is a place to eat cake, and a visit was generally a pretext for satisfying one's hunger rather than one's thirst. Traditionally, the choice of tea was limited to the most basic Earl Grey, Darjeeling, or Ceylon varieties. But take a look around: scrumptious babas, cream puffs, and chocolate éclairs line the trolleys and windows. One is forced to conclude that Parisian tearooms are simply upscale patisseries. Or are they? Although the tradition endures at places such as Angelina on rue de Rivoli and Carette on place du Trocadéro, a new phenomenon has sprung up as Parisians have begun to take tea seriously and treat it in much the same way as they would fine wine. They are learning about the different plantations in Darjeeling, enthuse about green tea, and are fascinated by the complicated hierarchy attached to China tea. Unlike the Japanese, with their tea ceremony, Parisians are not interested in tea as some sort of metaphysical metaphor, nor do they associate it with a particular moment in the day, like the English with afternoon tea or the Russians with their samovars. Their approach—albeit in a more modest fashion—is more like that of the Chinese, anxious to recognize the source of a particular variety, to place it on a hierarchical scale, and to appreciate fully the specific characteristics of a particular tea or a particular grower. Two coinciding phenomena explain this sudden growth of interest in tea. First, the emergence of a genuine French *art du thé*, despite the fact that not a leaf is grown in the country. Second, the emergence of Paris, or rather the choice of Paris by certain Asian tea experts, as the Western outpost for the trade in high-quality teas from the leading markets in Hong Kong, Singapore, and Taipei.

MARIAGE FRÈRES

The Mariage Frères boutique on rue du Bourg Tibourg in the Marais is modeled on the interior of a nineteenth-century tea merchant. Its colonial ambience and heady aromas are integral to the art of tea à la française.

MARIAGE FRÈRES

*You can choose a tea here
to take home, or initiate
yourself into the mysteries
of this beverage in the tearoom
at the back where all the blends
in the boutique out front
are available for tasting.*

Is there a specifically French way of having tea? If there is, the credit must go to two foreigners, a Dutchman by the name of Richard Bueno, grandson of a plantation owner in Indonesia, and Kitti Cha Sangmanee, an aficionado of tea, as is common in his native Thailand. In the early 1980s, the two men discovered a wholesale tea merchant on rue du Cloître Saint-Merri by the name of Mariage Frères. The firm was run by Marthe Cottin, whose ancestor Henri Mariage had founded the business. Richard Bueno and Kitti Che Sangmanee were awed by the authentically timeless atmosphere of the strictly wholesale store—furniture impregnated with tea dust, old weighing scales, leather drawer pulls. They became friends with Marthe Cottin, who initiated them into the tea trade *à la française* and, considering them her true successors, subsequently sold them the business. Mariage Frères had been trading in teas from the finest gardens and blending them for the European market since the seventeenth century. The new owners kept the original wholesale store, but went one step further by opening a retail boutique on rue du Bourg Tibourg in the Marais neighborhood in 1985. They kept the furniture from the original premises that had so attracted them in the first place: wooden panels, tea chests, and memorabilia. For the first time, Paris had a wide selection of teas—some five hundred of them from thirty-six different countries. Because they knew their customers were likely to be largely ignorant of what they were buying, the partners paid particular attention to educating them, going so far as to produce a brewing chart giving the correct infusion times and temperatures for each variety. Parisians were bowled over by this. For the first time, somebody was talking about tea in a language they understood.

Mariage Frères, guided by its new owners, offered something to a sophisticated clientele that no teabag could match. Mariage Frères classified its five hundred teas into the finest "first flushes," garden teas that come from a distinct region, blended teas that combine different types of tea, and

aromatic teas that incorporate spices, flowers, fruits, or roots. In doing this, two distinct skills come into play. The first is akin to that of the vintner, who carefully selects and brings to fruition his wine; the second is that of a perfumer who combines flavors and aromas to produce an original result. The two partners were not content simply to create a pleasant environment around the old-fashioned countertops in their three boutiques. They were also the first to invite their customers to inhale the aroma of the tea directly from the tins in which it is stored, a gesture hitherto unknown in Paris.

As part of their gourmet approach, they have added a tearoom to their boutique on rue du Bourg Tibourg, not a patisserie, but a real dining area where

one can eat and drink at any time of the day. In so doing, they have changed the way Paris drinks tea. At the same time they have created a particularly Parisian attitude as to how and where tea should be drunk. No longer is it limited to accompanying cakes and pastries; tea can be consumed with savory dishes as well. Tea has become a possible accompaniment to every meal, from breakfast to dinner, not only an alternative to morning coffee but also to wine. This is not to say that France is on the verge of abandoning wine for tea. Rather that those who appreciate tea now recognize that the same sort of matches can be made between food and a beverage that has a character as universal as wine. Mariage Frères has published a book that contains two hundred original recipes that go well with tea. For that reason alone, it is fair to assert that Mariage Frères invented the "French art of tea." Dozens of similar Parisian teashops embrace the concept: Le Palais des Thés, Les Thés de Chine, La Maison de la Chine, Le Jardin des Voluptés, and Tch'a offer China teas; Chajin has Japanese teas; Chatura sells Ceylon teas; Les Comtes de Thé stocks the finest Darjeeling teas; Kusmi features Russian tea; Espace Art has Arab teas; and many others offer a small but excellent selection of high-quality teas. Mariage Frères' unique "French art of tea" has achieved international recognition with the opening of two tearooms in Tokyo, one in Kyoto, one in Kobe, and ten "corners" in Tokyo department stores.

Another sign of this change is the opening of a store specializing in rare and precious teas on rue Gracieuse behind the Pantheon, La Maison des Trois Thés. A plain storefront, a bell at the entrance, a subdued Ming-like décor, and a few tables is all there is on the ground floor. The real business is downstairs in the basement where seventeen tons of tea is stored in strictly controlled conditions. This is an important center in the international tea trade, and although private individuals are welcome, the majority of its customers are professionals and collectors from around the world. If further proof were needed of Paris's significance in the tea trade, Madame Tseng Yu Hui,

**LA MAISON
DES TROIS THÉS**
*At La Maison des Trois Thés,
Madame Tseng (above),
an undisputed tea expert,
holds court. The tea is prepared
according to traditional
Chinese methods and weighed
on antique scales, the boxes
marked only with ideograms.*

originally from China and one of the world's leading tea experts, has chosen Paris as her base. The role of the tea expert is important because unlike with wine, there is no *appellation contrôlée.* The reputation of a particular tea plantation—and the price of certain prestigious teas—depends in large part on the opinions of these experts who co-opt their members from a restricted circle of growers, traders, and recognized connoisseurs. Tseng Yu Hui belongs to all three of these circles. On her mother's side, she comes from a family of tea planters in Fujian where Oolong tea—a semi-fermented variety—is traditionally produced. Two hundred years ago, her ancestors were among the first to bring tea to Taiwan. Her family still owns a plantation producing one of the

best Oolongs, Jong Ding. It was in this atmosphere that Tseng Yu Hui grew up. In keeping with the family tradition, and in order to ensure an exclusive supply of the best teas, she has plantations in Taiwan and mainland China. Paradoxically, her experience as a trader began in Europe during the early 1990s, because nowhere could she find—particularly in Paris—the teas she had enjoyed during her youth. Five or six times a year, she goes to China and Taiwan where she chooses teas at their source. But she also deals in vintage teas, the famous *pu-erhs,* or oxidized teas, that age as well as—if not better than—the best Bordeaux wines. In Taiwan, Tseng Yu Hui has a list of some five hundred teas, and in Paris she offers teas that date to the early twentieth century. Prices for these teas can reach astronomical levels, often in the region of tens of thousands of dollars per kilo. But to appreciate them you need to be a genuine connoisseur, and it is here that one is drawn to the very Asian rituals of initiation, and not just initiation to tea. Early on, Tseng Yu Hui's instructors recognized her vocation. Apart from teaching her everything there was to know about tea, her family was told to develop her sensibilities and to this end she was trained in very specific domains, first in the traditional areas of Chinese medicine and calligraphy. Her artistic side was also pursued. In Tseng Yu Hui's case, this involved music—she became a solo clarinetist on the concert circuit. Her career brought her to Paris, where she discovered a world-class cultural capital and a society where the art of food was primordial. She recognized that from Paris she could orchestrate the revival of the ancient Chinese tea tradition, which had been sacrificed to the demands of the Communist revolution. By doing so, she would also raise the profile of tea in the West. La Maison des Trois Thés is her way of fulfilling both ambitions. Only time will tell if she has succeeded in making Paris the Western tea capital she envisages, but in the interim, make the most of this renaissance and let a thousand tea plants bloom.

**LA MAISON
DES TROIS THÉS**
*With its terra-cotta teapots,
great range of tea, and porcelain
cups and bowls, traditional
Chinese tea institutions have
been transplanted to the banks
of the Seine, much to the delight
of Paris's tea lovers*

CAFÉ VERLET

At the Café Verlet next
to the Palais Royal an
old-fashioned percolator
is still used to brew the coffee,
while the original clock keeps
ticking in a timeless setting.

Paris is the coffee capital of the world. No matter what time of the day or night, coffee is a fundamental part of Paris life whether drunk standing at the bar or sitting on a terrace watching the beautiful people go by. London has its pubs, with their beers and spirits; Rome its bars where you can drink coffee, but there you always knock it back quickly. Paris has cafés, and it is no coincidence that although these institutions also sell alcohol and soda, they bear the name of their most popular beverage. But Parisians increasingly complain about the quality of their preferred stimulant. While not striving to imitate the Italian *ristretto*, which they think is too strong and bitter, and rejecting what the Americans call coffee, which they consider too bland to be the real thing, they nonetheless recognize—not without a certain nostalgia—that their own coffee is no longer what it used to be. Just twenty years ago, the old *cona* machines, a paraffin-heated contraption where the coffee brewed in the upper part before dripping into the jug below, still reigned supreme in the former coal merchant cafés. This has been replaced by the infernal espresso machine, which overly concentrates the taste of the coffee, making it difficult to appreciate, and couples this with a noise like that of a steam engine. The *cona*, on the other hand, allows the full aroma of the coffee to be released, and nothing is better for those roasted mocha or Arabica beans than long, slow infusion far from contact with metal. Real coffee lovers have taken refuge in their own kitchens where they perpetuate the Parisian coffee tradition, and in doing so are helping to maintain an equally important Parisian custom that is inextricably linked with coffee, the art of conversation. In former times, at literary salons, whether at court or in town, a sharp wit was often looked down upon and Parisians were considered superficial. The eighteenth-century statesman and diplomat Talleyrand noted as an excuse for this national propensity to "speak without saying anything," that "the power of speech was given to man to hide his true thoughts." But he was quick to attribute to coffee all the virtues he most admired: "Black as the devil, as hot as hell, as pure as an angel, and as sweet as love."

CAFÉ VERLET

Where better to practice the art of conversation than in an old-fashioned coffeehouse where they roast the coffee on site. At the Café Verlet, wit and intelligence fill the air.

For perfect coffee, look no further than Café Verlet, situated not far from the Palais Royal on rue Saint-Honoré. Here, we see that Paris's coffee merchants have nonetheless managed to uphold their traditions. Or rather, that they have managed to rediscover their traditions, because it was only in 1965 that Pierre Verlet started selling a range of the finest Arabica coffees to restaurateurs, and subsequently to the general public. These days, it is Éric Duchossoy who has taken over the reins at Verlet, and he can boast about receiving his supplies from only the world's best coffee plantations, enabling him to offer coffee beans that originate from a single grower. And his approach is being imitated by the big coffee brands, which are increasingly pushing the origins of their beans as a distinguishing feature. While he doesn't make claims to practicing "fair trade," he respects many of its principles. During the coffee harvest from October to January, Duchossoy travels the world—from Cameroon to Laos, from Mexico to Panama—armed with a miniature coffee roaster and coffee maker so as to judge for himself the quality of that year's crop. That was how he found the Thong Set farm on the Bolovens Plateau in Laos. After the Indochina war, the Miaos went back to cultivating Arabica coffee bushes, which had originally been brought to this region, which is inherently suitable for the growing of coffee, by French botanists during the period of French colonial rule in Indochina. Further south, Duchossoy selects coffee from Memyo, a village in Myanmar where Arabica coffee was first introduced in the 1930s from Bourbon bushes originating on Karen Blixen's plantation in Kenya. In the Americas, he buys from the Torcaza farm in Panama, run by planters of Swedish descent who maintain the traditions of Scandinavian social democracy: a dispensary for the farm workers, schools for their children, recycling of the water that is used for washing the beans, and, of course, meticulous, not to say clinical, attention to detail when it comes to caring for the coffee bushes, be they of the *bourbon*, *tipica*, *catuia*, or *caturra* varieties. But Duchossoy's work is not limited to choosing the finest beans.

The beans have to be roasted, and they only reveal their true qualities after they have undergone this subtle process. Each roaster has his trade secrets, and each type of coffee needs roasting to a different point. Duchossoy puts it succinctly: "You have to adapt the roasting of each type of coffee to the final taste that it will have." Don't ask him how he knows what this taste is going to be, he cannot answer. Only through experience and innumerable experiments can he tell. What he does know, though, is how to avoid getting it wrong. Too fast a roasting and the result will be too acidic, so to avoid bitterness it is best to roast slowly. Too hot, and the result will be a "burnt" taste, which Duchossoy calls the "Italian taste" because of the Italian penchant for very strong,

LES COMPTOIRS RICHARD

Les Comptoirs Richard has helped to rekindle interest in traditional coffee roasting thanks to its contemporary décor and a range of products that includes not just coffee, but also coffeepots, specialty sugars, and chocolates. At the rue due Cherche Midi branch you can even taste teh coffee before buying it.

LES COMPTOIRS RICHARD

Here the origins of the coffees are clearly marked, and with grands crus *and interesting blends lying side by side, buying coffee has never been such a pleasure.*

almost bitter coffee. Yet the so-called German or American roasting methods that are supposed to reduce bitterness have a tendency to exacerbate it because the bean is only browned on the outside and the acidity remains inside. Duchossoy's roasting technique aims to achieve a perfect balance between acidity and bitterness and in doing so to release the essential oils that lie dormant in coffee beans so as to reveal the full range of aromas and taste sensations they contain. And that, it has to be said, is just what Parisians want from a coffee merchant.

For those who can't make the pilgrimage to rue Saint-Honoré, there is always the chance to have a good cup of coffee brewed according to the same principles at Les Comptoirs Richard. This century-old establishment has succeeded in winning a large number of Parisian cafés to its cause, and the result is excellent coffee. Nowadays, they also have five points of sale of their own in Paris. The one on rue du Cherche Midi, with its bags of coffee beans, range of coffeepots, and coffee paraphernalia, and an area to taste before you buy, is a distinctly pleasant place to visit. A strong smell of roasting coffee greets you as you enter. Attentive and well-trained staff is there to serve you from a large selection of guaranteed "pure" Arabica coffee from around the world: *maragogype* from Mexico, known as Liquidambar; huge beans with citrus overtones, which are surprisingly mild in flavor; Blue Mountain from Jamaica that is velvety and chocolaty to the taste; and mocha from Ethiopia with its complex aromas. Les Comptoirs Richard is also the source of blends such as Perle Noire, which contains Arabica beans from several sources, a blend that is now available on the terraces of many cafés throughout the city and which, in its own way, has helped to reconcile Parisians to both their city and their favorite drink.

Savory
Paris

Bread and cheese

When the women of Paris set off to demonstrate at Versailles on October 5, 1789, thereby forcing Louis XVI, Marie-Antoinette, and the young heir to the throne to decamp to the Tuileries, their initial objective had been to return with "the baker, the baker's wife, and the apprentice." Such was the importance of bread at the time of the ancien régime. It has been said that the events of July 1789 started off as a bread riot and turned into a revolution, due to the dearth of food in the preceding period and the high price of bread, an essential part of the French diet in the eighteenth century. Today, food is no longer scarce and bread is plentiful, but Parisians continue to complain: bread no longer tastes like it used to. Good bread is impossible to find, they say. If that is true, it is not for want of trying on the part of the great and the good who came up with the annual "Best Baguette In Paris" prize.

Today, there are still more than 1,300 traditional *boulangeries-pâtisseries* in Paris, though ten years ago there were 6,000. Yet bread consumption has increased slightly over that period, from 150 grams per inhabitant per day to 163 nowadays. So should one believe Parisians when they complain about the state of bread? Yes, if what they are talking about is the industrial bread that is sold in supermarkets, which goes rubbery after a day on the shelf. But for genuine bread lovers—and there are many of them—a detour to another district, or even a trip to another part of the city, in search of a real baguette or an authentic loaf of bread is worth the trouble. And they are well rewarded for their efforts, because paradoxically, although the baking industry is undoubtedly in crisis, at the quality end of the market, bread has never been so good, whether you look at the variety on offer or the care that is paid to how it is made. While bread may not yet be a luxury, for many Parisians the address of a good bakery is, and one that they pass to one another by word of mouth, like a precious secret. The names of some of these elite bakers are as much a password to quality as those of any of the master chefs and patissiers.

POILÂNE

Welcome to Pierre Poilâne's historic boutique on rue du Cherche Midi, near the Saint-Germain area. For many years, Parisians have lined up to buy their bread here, not because there was any particular shortage, but because here they could be sure to find the very best quality bread.

POILÂNE

Poilâne is also the place to come to for delicious little butter cookies, whether for a quick mid-morning bite to stave off your hunger before lunch, or with tea as an afternoon snack. While waiting, take a look at the collection of still lifes of bread displayed on the walls (facing page).

This is unquestionably true of Poilâne. A food critic once wrote that Pierre Poilâne and his son Lionel were to baking what Gaston Lenôtre was to pastry and Paul Bocuse to restaurants. Following World War II, Parisians had had enough of black bread: it had been their staple during the Occupation and with liberation they longed for bread that was white, with a loose and springy crumb and a crust as golden as the future they were looking forward to. To satisfy them, many bakers produced a baguette that appeared perfect, but only on the outside. To give their bread an extra lift and make the crumb airy —which consumers took to be a sign of quality, so used had they been to the hard and compact bread of the war years— they added raising agents that resulted in a tasteless, neutral baguette lacking in aroma and a precursor of the industrial baguette to come. It was this baguette that became the norm and, like white bread had been in former times, was synonymous with the good life and a harbinger of better times to come.

In short, it was bread for the rich, bread to make you dream. At his bakery on rue du Cherche Midi, which he opened in 1932, Pierre Poilâne took a different approach to bread making. For Pierre, bread had to be made with stone-ground flour that was blackish-brown in color and slightly oily from the crushed wheat germ, it needed to rise using a natural leavening agent and then be baked in a wood-fired oven. In keeping with tradition, he refused to make baguettes, preferring instead to produce a hefty round loaf that would keep in the larder for several days. The result is the spectacular round loaf that weighs in at 1.9 kilograms (4.2 pounds), big enough for a family, sitting in the shop window, glowing like the sun. First to be drawn to this sun were the artists who populated the area around Poilâine's *boulangerie* situated not far from the École des Beaux-Arts. The artists were usually poor, and Pierre Poilâne's bread consistently nutritious, so it was not long before he began exchanging his bread for paintings and over time he succeeded in amassing a collection that depicts bread in all its glory. The works are still on show in the back of the shop, and while not all masterpieces—far from it—their presence is testament to the strength of the link between Poilâne bread and art. Against the odds, the artists in Saint-Germain-des-Prés succeeded in making *pain Poilâne* fashionable. The apotheosis of this synergy between the arts and crafts is the furniture that Pierre's son Lionel made from bread under the supervision of Salvador Dalí. The chandelier is still hanging in the shop. Little by little, the Poilânes's reputation continued to grow. Besides the original bakery on rue du Cherche Midi, a larger production facility was added in a converted farm in the suburb of Clamart. This supplied the twenty or so distributors of Poilâne

LE MOULIN DE LA VIERGE

The façade of the Moulin de la Vierge, on avenue du Suffren near the École Militaire, dates from 1900 and illustrates the traditions associated with bread in France. The silhouette of the woman sowing evokes the much later image of Marianne, icon of the French Republic, a secular goddess who for years adorned the French franc. The bread from the Moulin de la Vierge is distinctly nutritious, as it is made using only organic flour (facing page).

bread in Paris. But the methods used to make the bread didn't change. Poilâne began to export their bread during the 1970s, and you can now find it in the U.S., Japan, Hong Kong, and, of course, throughout Europe. *Pravda*, the official organ of the Soviet Communist Party, once published a report on the lines that formed outside the bakery on the rue du Cherche Midi: a sign, it claimed, of the shortage of bread in the West. In 1982, having been forced to leave Clamart, the Poilâne business—because at this stage it had gone from being a bakery to being a sizable business in its own right—built a brand new production facility in Bièvre, between Paris and the wheatfields of Beauce. While the architecture might be modern, the production area is fitted out exactly like an eighteenth-century bakery might have been: twenty-four wood-fired ovens and a similar number of preparation areas are organized along traditional lines. A crane located in the middle of the ovens rotates to distribute wood and the flour that is stored in four huge silos arrives directly into each kneading trough by means of a pneumatic system. In an era where modern bakeries make soulless bread in increasingly large quantities, Lionel Poilâne succeeded in inventing a "retroactive" factory that manages to combine the best of modern technology with traditional bread making methods. A visit to the rue du Cherche Midi bakery is like a trip to a museum: the sales assistants are dressed in linen smocks and the pale wood décor is permeated with the warm, slightly pungent aroma of the fresh bread that is produced here daily. The range of breads on sale has not changed since the 1970s: the round loaf that still carries the bakers monogram, the walnut bread rolls, and the deliciously yellow sandwich bread (only on sale in this location because "it doesn't travel well") are all made from wheat flour, while the rye bread is particularly appreciated for its smoothness and the touch of sweetness that comes from a rye-based leaven that incorporates a tiny amount of wheat flour. By preserving traditional methods, Lionel and Pierre Poilâne revolutionized and transformed an entire profession. Following the tragic 2003 accident in which Lionel was killed, the task of continuing this tradition has passed to his daughter Appolonia.

Bread is intrinsically linked to social history, and that is particularly true of Paris. In its quest for modernization, Paris nearly lost its baking tradition. It called for a Pierre and Lionel Poilâne to preserve that tradition. As part of its reaction against the excesses of modern urbanization, the city has welcomed and encouraged those "bread makers" who strive to satisfy the demands of a population that is particularly attached to its lifestyle. The story of the Moulin de la Vierge, a bakery

LE MOULIN DE LA VIERGE

*The traditional interior
has been preserved at the
Moulin de la Vierge, on
rue Vercingétorix, and
in all the other outlets of
this typically Parisian bakery.*

LE MOULIN DE LA VIERGE

*The panels that decorate
the walls and ceiling of this
bakery reflect how for Parisians
bread and love are inextricably
linked. In need of a little
tenderness? The Moulin de la
Vierge has delicious* viennoiserie
*breakfast pastries to be eaten
alone or with the one you love.*

on rue Vercingétorix next to the railway tracks that lead to Montparnasse station, is a good example of this trend. Difficult as it is to imagine today, in the middle of the 1970s a posse of technocrats came up with a plan to run a series of highways through the center of Paris culminating in a central junction at Notre Dame. Skyscrapers would be dotted here and there, in case the highways did not succeed in making Paris—the City of Light after all—"modern" enough. In 1975, the area around this antique bakery was demolished in preparation for the massive public works to come. But like the village that held out against the Romans in the Asterix cartoons, this typical old boutique with its beautiful façade painted on glass was spared the wrecker's ball.

The culture minister, in a wise move, gave the building protected status, though no bread had been baked in its ovens for the previous five years. Basile Kamir was one of a handful of activists determined to prevent the bulldozers from doing their work. A childhood friend of the founder of the Virgin empire, Richard Branson, and a concert promoter in his own right, Basile Kamir decided to buy the historic monument. It was said that in the Middle Ages a flour mill had stood on the site, and that the Virgin Mary had freed the miller from a pact he had made with the devil. Basile Kamir used the shop to sell records, but locals who visited constantly complained of the disappearance of all of the area's bakeries, so he decided to start selling Poilâne bread alongside his records. The Moulin de la Vierge had begun a return to its roots. To get over the thorny issue of where to plant their highway, the planners proposed taking down the boutique and building it elsewhere. But a traditional wood-fired oven is not as easy to take down and reassemble as is a façade, and once in use its destruction is forbidden. To foil the planners' intentions once and for all, Basile Kamir ended up resuscitating the oven and making the store a bakery once again. He called on the services of Monsieur de Collogne, a master baker of the old school, to get things going again, and because Basile Kamir was an environmentalist, he made sure only to use organic flour in his breads. Many legal battles and one hunger strike later—ironic for a baker—Basile Kamir succeeded in saving the Moulin de la Vierge, and in the process saved Paris from the planned highways that would have disfigured the city irreparably. An incredible but true story with a satisfactory outcome and one that would have been impossible to make up. The concert promoter turned baker has spawned seven other outlets in the city all of which use the same techniques as Poilâne and organic ingredients that produce excellent bread. The activist has turned into a successful baker, and Parisians are undoubtedly better off as a result.

Quality baking is not necessarily synonymous with a rigid adherence to the past. Lionel Poilâne's production facility is evidence of that. Two other bakers, each in his own way, illustrate this: Éric Kayser and Francis Holder, founder of the Paul group. Éric Kayser is the rising star of a new breed of Paris baker. Parisians enjoy labeling as "new" anything that deviates from the ordinary, opens up new paths of discovery, or creates new sensations, even if genuine innovation is not always in evidence. But Éric Kayser's reputation—he is the first "star" baker since Lionel Poilâne—is founded on a genuine innovation and an approach that is truly revolutionary. Kayser's breads, despite the wide variety of flours used and varieties on offer, share a common consistent quality that is unaffected by weather conditions or the hand that makes them. This is not to say that his breads are uniformly the same. Rather, that whether it is a country loaf or one made of buckwheat, rye, or a combination of ten different grains, or even just a simple baguette, they all have the same qualities that, according to Kayser, are essential for good bread: an appetizing color both in the crust and the crumb, a crusty outside and soft inside, and above all the irregularly shaped air pockets that are the sign of handmade bread. How does he achieve this "handmade" quality while ensuring that each loaf is consistently perfect? By carefully introducing technology into the process at the right moment. Éric Kayser grew up in the family bakery in Lure in the Haute Saône region. As part of his training he undertook an age-old system of apprenticeship—the *compagnons de devoir*—that took him to work with the best bakers in France until he graduated under the soubriquet *Francomtois le Décidé*. Very early in his career he discovered a vocation as a teacher and from Mexico to Dubai, from Stockholm to Toronto, he has taught bread making while continually observing and learning everywhere he goes. With his vast experience and from his contacts in the food industry—in particular with Patrick Castagna, an engineer specialized in bread making—he came up with the idea of a machine that would automate

ÉRIC KAYSER

The bread at Éric Kayser's is a paradox: each loaf is different but each the same. The secret of how to achieve this uniform individuality lies in a special machine, the fermentolevain, *which controls the release of the acids in the yeast leaven. The rows of chairs (facing page) in the boulevard Malesherbes branch invite the shopper to stop for a little treat. The branch on rue de l'Ancienne Comédie behind Saint-Germain-des-Prés also has a seating area.*

ÉRIC KAYSER

Éric Kayser's bakeries
double as tearooms.
Come and enjoy a sandwich
or a pastry, the financiers,
small almond sponge cakes
(facing page), are a hit.

the most delicate part of the bread making process: controlling the fermentation of the leaven. Why do bakers not sleep at night? The main reason why their hours are so out of synch is that they are obliged to watch over how the leaven ferments and ensure it does not over ferment or become too "thin," releasing unpleasant acetic acids that would result in a vinegar-like taste in the bread. The aim is to have a *leaven* with just the right balance of acids that complement each other, resulting in a pleasant combination of aromas and tastes ranging from acidic to lactic to honey that are the hallmark of good bread. Éric Kayser invented the machine and had it made industrially. In 1994, his *fermentolevain* machine was put on sale to the general consternation of his professional brethren who attached an almost mystical quality to this aspect of their art and for whom no machine could possibly replace the baker's own senses of smell, taste, touch, and sight. In order to convince them, Éric Kayser became his own first customer. Thanks to his artistry, and because he knew how to set up his *fermentolevain* to get optimal results—at this stage nothing can replace the baker's eye, nose, hand, and palate—he started producing bread that became the talk of the town.

In his first boutique on rue Monge in the Latin Quarter, Éric Kayser also had the idea to let his customers see the production process from beginning to end from the store floor. Behind the counter, a window looks onto the preparation and baking area, where bakers slide the loaves and baguettes into and out of the hot oven. A front row seat at the birth of the bread one is about to buy. Not content to innovate only in the technical aspects of bread making, Éric Kayser was also supremely creative in the range of breads that he came up with. Varieties such as turmeric and hazelnuts, poppy seeds, olives, Beaujolais and cheese, seaweed, prune and bacon have made their way from the tables of the great Paris restaurants into people's homes and bread is now eaten as a gastronomic delicacy in its own right.

For Francis Holder also, it was important that his customers could see the bread coming out of the oven. Originally from Lille, he has built up the largest chain of bread shops in France, with forty in Paris alone. The Paul chain of bakeries are recognizable by their distinctive black and gold storefronts, their well-stocked window displays that are changed four times daily, the friendly atmosphere that reigns and the staff dressed like baker's apprentices of old, topped off with the traditional *faluche* hat. They have become an integral part of the urban landscape, and one could be forgiven for thinking they had been there forever. In actual fact they first appeared during the early 1990s. Holder comes from a family of bakers with roots in the north going back four generations to 1889. The Paul bakery in Lille was

renowned for its Viennese-style breads. In 1958, when Holder took over from his father, France was on the brink of a revolution in how it was to do its shopping with the imminent arrival of the supermarket. Bakers were faced with a dilemma: either they went the way of other small businesses and let themselves be absorbed by the new giants with the risk that their bread would become just another industrial product, or they could follow the French in their exodus to the new shopping centers and continue to provide the traditional bread that their customers still craved. Holder chose to develop genuine bakeries in areas with close proximity to the supermarkets that surround France's cities and to combine a strong brand identity with a guarantee of first-rate quality. They are like oases of authenticity in a desert of mass-produced uniformity. Paul bakeries and outlets are now to be found in train stations and airports as well as shopping centers, and while Paul may have taken on the attributes of a brand name, it has nonetheless succeeded in retaining the traditional working methods that make French bread unique. The number of Paul bakeries in Paris is more a sign of how a traditional bakery has successfully adapted to modern conventions than the triumph of a carefully constructed marketing concept. And Parisians are delighted with the result, something which would not have been possible had the bread not been up to scratch. In this respect, Holder never neglected what was always the strong point of his shops. His intention has always been to give to his customers what they really want. Which is why he places so much emphasis on ingredients, in particular the flour: he uses a rustic winter variety of wheat, grown according to sound farming principles, that has no additives or preserving agents, is rich in wheat germ, and is spread out and left to mature for thirty days before being milled. It takes seven hours to make a loaf of Paul bread, the same time it took Francis Holder's ancestors all those years ago. The difference is that in order to keep up with the cravings of his Parisian clientele he has 142 varieties of bread on offer, starting with the classic Paul loaf made of Camp Rémy flour. This is then "rolled out" into loaves with names like "*pistolet*," "*paulette*," "*faluche*," "*ficelle*," "*flute*," "*chapata*," "*épi*," "*couronne*," and "*polka*" that are flavored with sesame or poppy seeds, bacon, onion, olives, and walnuts, making forty-two varieties of bread from a single basic dough. Then there is the "*benoiton*," a whole wheat roll perfect for a little snack or a romantic dinner and available in eight varieties: apricot, date, fig and raisin, raisin, hazelnut and cinnamon, olive oil, green olive, and black olive. Finally, there is the organic bread that uses only a natural leaven made from stone-ground flour containing coarse sea salt from the Guérande and no pesticides. Francis Holder has made the best of good French bread available to Parisians and they are grateful to him for it.

PAUL

Aux Tortues on boulevard Haussmann is the flagship for Paul's operations in Paris. The window display (following pages) changes four times a day: breads and breakfast pastries in the morning, sandwiches and hot dishes at lunchtime, pastries and cakes in the afternoon, and finally, more breads in the evening.

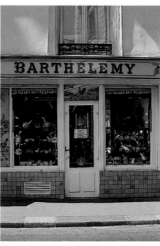

BARTHÉLEMY

The boutique on rue de Grenelle doesn't look anything special from the outside, but step inside and you enter one of the doyens of the capital's cheese shops. Follow the advice of Monsieur and Madame Barthélémy and you will only buy what is in season. Facing page: Delicious little goat cheeses on sticks.

Where there is bread, there has to be cheese, said writer Colette, quoted by the no less great cheese merchant Pierre Androuët. In one of his many books on cheese he wrote, "Paris has all the cheeses, the soft, the bitter, the tangy, the strongly fermented, the ones that age in the cellars of France and the ones that come from afar. None lack customers. What is missing are the women, the people who know something about cheese. Women are fond of cheese but they have fallen prey to an obsession with slimness." Is this sad state of affairs still true? In the French capital—and by extension the cheese capital—the number of cheese merchants and shops selling dairy produce (known as *BOFs* for Beurre, Oeufs, Fromage) has fallen drastically, and it is true that women continue to be obsessed with their weight, but cheese lovers can gather some reassurance from the fact that the fat content of cheese is not nearly so high as they might think. Measurement of the fat content of cheese is taken from a dry extract, in other words on what is left over after all the water has been removed. So a *fromage blanc* cream cheese with a 40 percent fat content in reality is composed of only 8 percent fat and a camembert with a 45 percent fat content contains 25 percent. The industry is waiting for a ruling due shortly from the European Union that will allow them to display the real fat content on their products. While they wait for this to happen, they can console themselves with the knowledge that while women may be eating less cheese overall, what they are eating is likely to be of better quality than in the past, made from unpasteurized milk and perhaps bearing an *appellation d'origine contrôlée* label, guaranteeing its contents.

Pierre Androuët, who in the early 1970s had trouble in convincing people of the superiority of these "country" cheeses, would be pleased to note that he has won the battle for public opinion and that authentic, unpasteurized, strong-tasting cheese has become the benchmark for quality in the eyes and mouths of Parisiennes and French women in general.

This "ideological" battle was won by a few elite cheese merchants, among them Androuët, whom we have already mentioned, Marie-Anne Cantin, Marie Quatrehomme, and Roland Barthélémy. Barthélémy has led what amounts to a crusade to rehabilitate the profession of cheese merchant and have it recognized through a special *Meilleur Ouvrier de France* (literally, best craftsman in France) competition for the profession. In 1997, he achieved his goal, and in 2000 the first four candidates received this prestigious, state-recognized award. In 2004, the number of candidates had increased to six, a sign of the importance of emulating one's peers in

a profession such as this. But what can one expect of a *Meilleur Ouvrier de France* cheese merchant? Roland Barthélémy describes as follows the ambition that must drive a hopeful candidate: "He has to make the role of the cheese merchant intrinsic to gastronomy as a whole." As for what the jury looks for: "A *Meilleur Ouvrier de France* cheese merchant should be capable of suggesting combinations of cheese with various dishes and wines, without trespassing on what is ultimately the preserve of the chef, and also propose subtle marriages of tastes, like for example Roquefort with gingerbread or fruit. He should be able to create flavored goat cheeses or blend radically different cheeses like a Coulommiers that has a bloomy rind,

with a creamy truffled Mascarpone." In short, they are looking for creativity. Barthélémy himself is a keen promoter of this sort of creativity. Since 1971, cheese lovers have been making the pilgrimage to his shop on the corner of rue de Grenelle and boulevard Raspail in the heart of what used be known as the Faubourg Saint-Germain. As you squeeze into his tiny 150 square foot boutique where only cheeses in season are on display, it is hard to imagine that the cellar extends for three times that surface area and contains up to three hundred varieties of cheese at different stages of maturity. And of course throughout France—in Bauges, Salers, Roquefort, Fort des Rousses, or Doubs—cheese is waiting in various stages of development in dairies and caves before being shipped here. His own creations are reason alone for a visit, like the little terrine of fresh goat cheese with its alternating layers of cheese and fresh tomato that are doused in a *coulis* of fresh tomato, basil and *tapenade* (black olive paste). Then there is the fabulous Mont d'Or trussed up in a spruce-wood corset to prevent the cheese from oozing out; the Barthélémys remove the rind from on top so that all you have to do is plunge a spoon into the creamy mass inside. And they are always on hand to offer advice on how to get away from the time-honored cheeseboard and move on to something more gastronomically exciting, like mixing little balls of bleu d'Auvergne with walnuts, Chaource with yellow plums, or Ossau-Iraty with cherries.

If Roland Barthélémy is the high priest of Paris cheese, then Marie-Anne Cantin, in her shop on the far side of the Champs de Mars, is its high priestess. Together with her husband Antoine Dias, this passionate and vivacious woman has become an ambassador for French cheese throughout the world and for cheeses from the rest of the world in Paris. In Japan, she has outlets in Tokyo and Hiroshima and from her cellars in the seventh arrondissement over 450 pounds (200 kilos) of cheese are sent each week to the land of the rising sun. As supplier for twelve years to the presidential

BARTHÉLÉMY

Lose your heart to a delicious Brie. Anyone who is anyone comes to this little old-fashioned cheese shop that also sells every possible cheese accessory you can imagine.

MARIE-ANNE CANTIN
*At Marie-Anne Cantin's,
behind the Champ de Mars,
you will find tiny fresh goat
cheeses, perfect for a little
snack, or Camembert, that
she ripens herself, made from
unpasteurized milk*

palace, the National Assembly, and the Senate she has also been responsible for generating awareness of French cheese among visiting dignitaries. Alongside the traditional Brie, Comté, and Roquefort you might expect, she is happy to display English Stilton, Cabrales from Asturias, real Greek Feta, and Queijo Serra da Estrella from Portugal. Cantin is delighted to introduce Parisians to cheeses from what she calls "our European cousins." Her boutique has become an obligatory staging post for tourists to Paris and is present in every guide book to the city. There isn't a moment in the day when an American or Japanese tourist cannot be found admiring the huge choice of cheeses that fill the shelves of her boutique. Cantin welcomes everyone, tourist and loyal customer alike, with the same smile and is happy to explain why France has the best cheese in the world: the diversity of its countryside and climate, its mountains and the seasonality of its cheese that depends on the three best periods in the year for milk—the sprouting of the grass (the germination), the first flowering of the pastures, and the second growth of grass. But she is not afraid to gently rebuke her customers when they don't choose one of the European cheeses of which she is such a champion in their selection. The mayor of Paris, Bertrand Delanoë, has been spied enjoying a two-year-old Comté in her cellar. Hardly surprising, when, according to Cantin, this is the ideal age for this hard cheese. The privilege of visiting the immaculately maintained cellar—is strictly in keeping with the latest hygiene regulations—is reserved for the lucky few, but as soon as you open the door of one of the four cold rooms that she uses to ripen her cheeses, your senses are flooded with the aromas that burst forth from within. As a gastronome herself, Cantin is happy to dispense useful advice to those who buy her products and to suggest delicious recipes that will add a new dimension to your enjoyment of cheese. In winter, she suggests soup of milk and Roquefort; in spring, canapés of goat cheese with paprika, cumin, and mixed herbs (tarragon, chives, chervil); in summer, Fontainebleau with strawberries and lavender flowers; or in fall, hare with Comté. All are testament to the abiding creativity and intelligence of this woman who has devoted herself to a fundamental component of fine French cuisine.

Fine food stores

Because of Paris's geographic location, butter has traditionally been the substance of choice for cooking, though lard occasionally makes an appearance. "Cooked with butter" is synonymous with good cooking, matched only for true gourmets by "cooked with cream." Neutrality has always been favored when it comes to cooking oil, which is why peanut oil is mixed with vinegar to form vinaigrette or as a substitute for animal or dairy fat when cooking. Olive oil used only to be of marginal importance in Paris kitchens, perhaps used on a tomato salad as a reminder of a past Mediterranean holiday or to evoke thoughts of a forthcoming trip to the Côte d'Azur. What is more, it had a reputation for being heavy and not standing up well to cooking, in short, being difficult to digest. Added to that was the catastrophic frost in the winter of 1956 that killed almost two-thirds of all the olive trees in Provence. So there was no objective reason why Paris should play a central role in any renewed interest in the so-called "Mediterranean diet" and in olive oil in particular. Yet it was from Paris that olive oil launched its onslaught and achieved its ultimate victory in the culinary world. Several factors were at work in making this happen. One was the role of chefs like Alain Ducasse who had achieved success on the Côte d'Azur and then came to Paris looking for further glory. The role of nouvelle cuisine in general was also important, with its emphasis on simply prepared ingredients and the use of the right olive oil as an accompaniment to certain dishes, particularly fish. But nothing would have happened were it not for the initiative of a certain number of individuals whose pioneering spirit helped olive oil achieve the status it now holds in Parisian homes and restaurants.

First to come to mind is Olivier Baussan, founder of Oliviers & Co. Before him, Paris had no boutiques specializing in olive oil, with the exception of L'Olivier on rue de Rivoli, that was more like an embassy of southern France in Paris than a shop, and which rather than setting out to educate the locals, was a Parisian outpost for those expatriates from the south of France who remained not a little suspicious of the dietary habits prevalent in their newly adopted city. Baussan's target was the native

OLIVIERS & CO
At the rue Lévis outlet, not far from the Parc Monceau, customers can taste various oils before buying them and decide which goes best with pasta, fish, or salad.

Parisian, and he set about educating his audience about a product which until his arrival had been relatively unknown in Paris. At the start of the 1990s this connoisseur of the Mediterranean (he also developed the concept behind the Occitane chain of stores) started choosing his suppliers based on the criteria that he wanted his new stores to promote: an identifiable region of production that had a reputation for the quality of their oils; olives were to be harvested by hand, no case could exceed twenty kilograms (forty-four pounds), and the journey from olive grove to where the oil would be extracted was not to be more than one or two hours; finally, pressing was to take place at specified times either in the owners' own mill or using traditional small stone mills, and the resulting oil was to be stored in a container appropriate to such a carefully made product. His conditions were draconian. Of the three hundred oils that he tastes each year he selects only thirty or so for sale.

Baussan first started looking for oils in Italy, then moved on to Spain and Provence. Today, Oliviers & Co. offers oils from Greece, Lebanon, and Portugal—where Baussan has bought his own olive grove in order to apply to himself the conditions he imposes on others. But the undoubted strength of the nine Paris boutiques is the quality of the information they dispense on the products they sell. Olivier Baussan has noticed how tastes have changed over time with a trend away from the fruity and more mature oils to more delicate, lighter oils with complex, subtle aromas. Informative labels on the bottles and cans tell the consumer not just about the nutritional value of the oil and where it comes from, but also the variety of olive used and the date it was harvested. Tasting notes accompany each product on sale. The result is that a product, about which only ten years ago Parisians knew hardly anything, has become a fixture at any festive occasion and the favorite oil of any self-respecting gourmet. And what started in Paris is now a worldwide phenomenon: Oliviers & Co. has branches in Brussels, London, New York, Boston, and Rio de Janeiro. Baussan has helped to bring olive oil out of the cultural ghetto that associated it with a particular Mediterranean ethnic origin and made it the oil of choice, an oil that is synonymous not just with eating well, but also with eating healthily.

Other boutiques specialized in olive oil have opened in Paris as a result: Allicante on boulevard Beaumarchais on the edge of the Marais, Le Monde des Olives on rue Laugier, and La Maison de l'Olive on rue Ampère. These stores specialize in olive oil from individual growers or small-scale producers and have given Parisians the possibility of discovering ever more esoteric oils and delving further into regional tastes and flavors.

Apart from olive oil, Paris has begun to show an interest in other oils that were common to rural society in the period preceding the agricultural revolution of the twentieth century. Before it became available on every supermarket shelf, oil was a rare—if indispensable—commodity that was used not just in preparing food, but also in lubricating machinery. Every region produced its own oil from whatever was grown locally: olives, if that was what was available, but also almonds, argan, colza, hazelnut, walnut, pine-nut, pistachio, and sesame. Some of these oils—argan, for example—are of North African origin. Others have been pressed in France since time immemorial.

Anne Leblanc is from a long line of oil millers. For four generations—since 1878 to be precise—the Leblanc family have owned an oil mill in the Saône et Loire region where the local farmers could bring their walnuts and colza to be pressed. At that time, such mills were common in France. Now only a few remain, and the Leblanc family's mill is one of those to have maintained the traditional working methods. While production methods may not have changed much, distribution has changed considerably. The renewed interest in oil as an ingredient in serious cooking has opened up new perspectives for those craftsmen concerned with quality. While Anne Leblanc's brothers Jean-Charles and Jean-Michel have continued to press their oil in the old-fashioned way, their sister has opened a tiny boutique on rue Jacob, between L'École des Beaux-Arts and the rue de Buci market, where connoisseurs can procure those oils which they would be forgiven for thinking had disappeared. The oils served up here are pure extracts of the original fruit, because the oils at Leblanc are simply decanted directly into the bottle, never filtered. The flavor is all the more intense for doing so. And in the same way as Oliviers & Co. set the scene for Paris's claim to olive oil capital of the world, who knows but that in time Leblanc, from its postage-stamp size boutique might well do the same for colza, hazelnut, or walnut oil.

Another typically local product that is in the process of receiving a gastronomic benediction in Paris is the *jamón ibérico* known more generally as *jabugo*, *pata negra,* and *bellota*. This ham is produced from the Iberian pig, a descendant of the wild boar that is reared in the oak forests of Estremadura and more generally all across the southwestern Iberian Peninsula. The black legged creature has the distinction of storing the oil secreted by acorns directly in its muscles, resulting in a highly distinctive taste. For obscure reasons linked to health and hygiene, this type of ham was banned in France until ten years ago. It is left to dry for anything between 15 and 48 months, the quality of the drying process being a gauge of the quality of the finished product. Since making its

LEBLANC

In their earthenware pots, the oils at Leblanc are a reminder of times when oil served many purposes, not just for cooking but also for oiling machinery and lighting. Nowadays, however, their oils from a wide variety of fruits and plants serve only one purpose: to please the palate.

BELLOTA BELLOTA

In a quiet backstreet off the Champs de Mars an impressive range of Spanish cured hams catches the eye. Bellota Bellota recognized the gastronomic possibilities of these hams, and the menu here will initiate you into the mysteries of the various types of pata negra, *which differ in taste according to origin and length of curing time.*

DA ROSA

*"Da Rosa—Épicier" is what
this institution on rue de Buci
likes to call itself and in so
doing renews a tradition
where "grocers" sold only the
very best of everything.
Spanish hams come from
the village of Guijuelo in
the south of the province
of Salamanca. A selection of
mustards line the window.*

first appearance in Paris, it has become the latest fad and is credited with every possible virtue under the sun. While it is reckoned to have the same cardiovascular benefits as olive oil, the main reason for its popularity lies in its appeal to all the senses: a puzzling aroma that on closer inspection reveals acorn oil, and a deep, intense flavor marked by a suaveness on the tongue and just a hint of saltiness. The fine-foods stores that brought this delicacy to Paris understood that if they were to interest people in it they would need to give them the opportunity to taste it, and in realizing this they launched—or rather, relaunched—a fashion, that of proposing a menu using the products on sale in the store.

Bellota Bellota near the Champs du Mars has opened a restaurant where you can taste a variety of hams on the same plate; on the terrace of Da Rosa, close to the rue de Buci market, you can sample Martin Raventos' Unico, which is to ham what Romanée Conti is to the Côte de Nuits in Burgundy. And if proof were needed that the vogue for *Jamon Iberico* has taken hold among a much larger audience, look no further than the *coin gourmand* delicatessen counter of Lafayette Maison which offers its own selection of hams from a refrigerated cellar in the basement. With this interest have come prices to match, though despite the levels they can sometimes reach, these do not yet seem to have inhibited the true amateur.

The phenomenon was much the same in the 1920s with caviar. After all, in Provence they used to make a *poutargue* from mullet roe that had been pressed, salted, and dried, and what is caviar if not the same thing made from sturgeon? It took two Armenian brothers from Russia, Melkou, and Mouchegh Petrossian, to "invent" caviar. Their "invention" was not so much to export a previously unknown comestible but to refine it so that it was acceptable to the sophisticated palates of 1920s Paris society. Until they came along, the sturgeon's roe had been pressed regardless of the variety of

fish from which it came. Recognizing that the roe from each species had its own specific taste and color, they distinguished between the different types of sturgeon—beluga, ossetra, and sevruga—and convinced Parisians that caviar should be eaten in a festive atmosphere, preferably accompanied by champagne or vodka. Nowadays it is the Petrossians' nephew Armen who runs the business. His ambition is for caviar to enter the gastronomic pantheon in its own right, which is why in 1999 he opened a restaurant above the famous boutique on rue de la Tour Maubourg. He already had one in New York, but perhaps caviar marries more easily with the cuisine there. Yet the Paris smart set didn't waste time in falling for the dishes that Armen Petrossian and his chef Sebastien Faré had concocted for them: Petrossian soft-boiled eggs, crispy from their breadcrumb coating, are topped with a mound of caviar to look like a Fabergé egg; fine sturgeon "cigars" are stuffed with caviar to resemble a saltimbocca. Recipes such as these add new dimensions to caviar, and in doing so give a new lease on life to Petrossian's fabled commodity.

The same formula has been applied to another product that Parisians are convinced they know all there is to know about but which in reality they have yet to discover fully, the truffle. Clément Bruno and Dominique Saugnac are intent on revealing all the nuances of the famous fungi, and with twenty years' experience as proprietor and chef, respectively, at Chez Bruno in Largues in the Var region, they are well placed to do so.

At the end of 2003 they opened their restaurant-cum-grocery Terre des Truffes on rue Vignon near the Madeleine where truffles are doled out according to the harvest and the seasons, because truffles are not just a winter food. True, the *tuber melanosporum* is the undisputed champion of the genre, rivaled only by its white cousin *tuber borchi*, also known as the *bianchetto d'Alba*. But Clément Bruno and Dominique Saugnac are keen champions of the rights of other truffles to

TERRES DE TRUFFES

Truffles of every sort and season—winter, summer, spring, and fall—can be found at Terre des Truffes. Parisians can rediscover the "black diamond" in all its guises at this boutique situated near the Madeleine.

PETROSSIAN

Preceding pages: There is no need to introduce Petrossian, famous worldwide for the caviar it "invented" in the 1920s, except to add that it also offers a fabulous selection of smoked wild salmon and eel, salmon roe, foie gras, and truffles. A paradise for the fortunate . . . and the fortuned.

IZRAËL

You can find anything at Izraël, in the Marais area—anything, that is, that can be eaten, drunk, or used to spice up or enliven a dish on the condition that you know what you are looking for and look for it yourself. An address for specialists.

stimulate our nostrils and make their way into the dishes we enjoy. *Tuber magnatum pico* from Piedmont; *tuber aestivum*, the summer truffle; *tuber uncinatum*, the Burgundy truffle; and the winter truffle *tuber mensentericum* prove that truffles are a year-round phenomenon.

At Terre de Truffes you can of course buy your truffles fresh or preserved, but if there is the slightest doubt as to which you want, why not try some of the delicious dishes that are available either to take out or eat in, such as scrambled eggs with truffles, truffled Brie de Meaux, and even a series of deserts where the complex aroma of truffle is married to a blancmange with apricot jam or a runny chocolate cake.

**LE COMPTOIR
DE LA GASTRONOMIE**
In the heart of Les Halles, the Comptoir de la Gastronomie maintains the tradition of fine food in this district, which the writer Émile Zola described in the nineteenth century as "the belly of Paris."

**LES PIPALOTTES
GOURMANDES**
On rue Rochechouart on the way to Montmartre, Les Pipalottes Gourmands is typical of a new generation of grocery stores that also serve as caterers.

It would seem as though all of Paris's fine food stores have given in to the craze of letting their customers eat on site. While the privileges accorded to innkeepers may have disappeared with the French Revolution—and even before with the encroachment of the café owners—no law today prevents a delicatessen from setting up a few tables and offering its wares for the gratification of its customers.

In this manner you can enjoy a slice of cloth-cooked foie gras at the Comptoir de la Gastronomie, one of the last gastronomic outposts remaining in the old market district of Paris or take a trip to Provence at the Pipalottes Gourmandes on rue Rochechouart on the way to Montmartre, where you can nibble on an open sandwich of sun-dried tomatoes and thyme drizzled with olive oil or knock back a mussel stuffed with pesto. The one fine foods store to resist this trend is the pleasantly topsy-turvy Izraël on the rue François Miron in the Marais, which continues to display its wares in bulk for all to see. While you might come here in search of some cassia, ginger or lime, you are likely to leave bearing a bag of red lentils or chickpea flour. Izraël is where Parisians come to find everything, from donuts just like you get in New York to the rhododendron-flavored honey typical of Aosta. It has to be pointed out that a trip to Izraël is like no other. With its thousands of articles literally crammed into every corner of the store and spilling off the shelves, it requires an initiation ceremony to understand it fully. If you are in search of a pleasant gastronomic diversion then this is not the place for you: Izraël is for specialists only. Do not expect to receive advice, only those able to identify what is on offer and who know for what it is used can really benefit from what is not so much a store as a treasure trove of food.

Paris in a glass

Famous and lesser-known wine merchants

Paris's love affair with wine goes back a long way. We know from the correspondence of the Emperor Julian—who made the city his capital—that the Romans were the first to plant vineyards in Paris, or Lutetia as it was then known, on the slopes of Suresnes, and on the hill of Montmartre. In October each year, the grape harvest is still the occasion for a party. In a fable from the Middle Ages, "The Battle of the Wines," the best wines from Paris—those from Montmorency, Mantes, Meulan, Pierrefitte and Argenteuil—hold their own against the finest growths from Champagne and Burgundy. Meudon, Sèvres, Issy, and Auteuil, suburbs of the city, were as renowned for their wines as Ay and Chablis. And while everyone knows that Paris is surrounded by five rivers, the Seine, the Aisne, the Marne, the Oise, and the Yonne, it can be said that a sixth river—of wine—has served the city since time immemorial, when wine from every region in France would flow into the capital to be stored in wooden barrels, first at the Place de Grève, now the place de l'Hôtel de Ville, and later in vast warehouses further downstream at Bercy. The city became France's most important center for trade in wine, in particular because it was home to the wine merchants who "followed the court," twelve suppliers granted the right to supply the king with wine. But the populace also had a healthy, not to say insatiable, appetite for wine, albeit of a lesser quality than that drunk at court. In suburbs such as Belleville, Auteuil, and Suresnes, wine was sold at half the price as that in the capital because it was not subject to the tariff imposed inside the city limits. As a result, *guinguettes*—out-of-town taverns—like the Ramponneau flourished. White wine (*la blonde*) and red wine —the darker the better—(*la négresse*) flowed freely, and while the quality may have left much to be desired, all that was asked of it was that it produce the required inebriation among its consumers.

For a long time wine was just another part of the Parisian diet; serious appreciation was reserved for an elite of connoisseurs. Parisians thought they knew all there was to know about wine because they drank so much of it. In fact they drank far too much of it: at the bistro, in restaurants, during meals, from breakfast to dinner and between meals too, to help them work better they claimed, whether it was the physical exertions of a stonemason or the mental efforts of a writer, wine was the

LA DERNIÈRE GOUTTE

At La Dernière Goutte Parisians are introduced to little-known wines from around France by an American!

LA DERNIÈRE GOUTTE

*Wine lovers gather to worship
at La Dernière Goutte,
in a cellar just a few yards
from the Place Furstenberg,
behind the church at
Saint-Germain-des-Prés.*

essential lubricant. And, of course, they drank it whenever they had a party. Suffice it to say that Parisians were not always the most discerning of wine drinkers. Indeed, up to thirty years ago, wine was still often bought in bulk and bottled at home, and since cellars in Paris apartment buildings are often small and not especially safe, it was best to drink it up quickly. Wine as an essential part of the art of living was only for the cosmopolitan privileged classes. While Paris might have been the wine capital of the world when measured by volume, its great rival London drank less, but what it drank was of better quality. This was the ultimate paradox: a city that was the capital of a country with the finest wines in the world was itself not particularly concerned about the quality of what it drank. While one should be careful about generalizing too much—the city's great restaurants were always well stocked with a plentiful supply of *grands crus*, and the gourmets that frequented these establishments knew how to marry a particular dish with just the right wine—most of the wine to be found in the city was of pretty poor quality.

But over time, with the rise in living standards and the move away from manual labor, new consumption patterns emerged. Wine ceased to be an essential component of every meal and became instead something to be relished and enjoyed with reference to its regional origins, indeed it came to be seen as the expression of a culture if not an entire civilization. Parisians began to take a greater interest in their national beverage. In their quest for greater knowledge of their country's traditions they were to be guided not by their fellow Frenchmen but by foreigners such as George Bardawil, an Englishman who in the early 1980s introduced Paris to the wine bar when he opened L'Écluse, the first of what was to become a chain. Anglo-Saxons have played a significant role in introducing Parisians to the discoveries they have made throughout France's regions, in the same way as they have been responsible for drawing their attention to every last vine of the Bordeaux and Champagne regions. Their own islands being devoid of any sort of vineyard, these eminent wine connoisseurs came in search of approbation. Or was it just that they wanted the approval and recognition of the French and Parisians in particular? For Michael Broadbent this was indeed the case: he was the first wine expert to organize an auction of fine wines at Sotheby's, and in 1971 the French government awarded him the Agricultural Order of Merit.

With this in mind, it is fitting that we begin our wine tour of Paris with another foreigner, Juan Sanchez. In his thirties and of Cuban-American origin, he originally came to Paris to study cookery at the École Ferrandi that has trained many of France's top chefs. Naturally, his interest in food led him to wine,

and in 1993 he opened Les Béoux in the heart of Saint-Germain-des-Prés. He moved premises, remaining in the same area, but changed the name to La Dernière Goutte. The new boutique is distinctly specialized and holds minimal stock, because with the sort of pragmatism for which Americans are renowned Juan Sanchez only sells the very best wines, though at reasonable prices, in the process earning the ultimate Parisian accolade—usually bestowed excitedly—of "excellent value for money." Many have tried the same formula, but few have succeeded as well as La Dernière Goutte. Because he was not born with the genetic tendency to vacillate only between Bordeaux and Burgundy that affects so many Parisians, Juan Sanchez chose to promote lesser-known wines that were beginning to make rapid advances in quality but were as yet unknown outside their regions: Corbières, Faugères, Coteaux du Roussillon, and Languedoc are all from the far south and their reputation in the capital had been marked by a quality in the past that was not always what it should have been, but Parisians have since come to love these wines for their intensity. As he continued his journey up the Rhone, Sanchez came across some of the better known wines but continued to find here and there, in Savoy and Jura—as well as already established regions such as Beaujolais, Alsace, and Champagne—winemakers producing the sort of wine he liked. Marcel Lapierre, André Osterag, and Anselme Selosse were not the stars they have since become when they first brought their wines to La Dernière Goutte for the tasting sessions that were organized there. This astute American has discovered a rich stream of wine for his local clientele, and it took an outsider, passionate about his latest discoveries to forge a lasting link between a highly demanding public and the avant-garde of French wine. After World War II, Saint-Germain-des-Prés became known for its basements where one danced existentialist be-bop. Nowadays, it is wine that provides the atmosphere in those same cellars.

Of course it is not just foreigners who have helped reveal new French wines. Les Caves Augé has been around since 1850 and run by Marc Sibard since 1988. Located on boulevard Haussmann in the heart of bourgeois Paris, Les Caves Augé never had difficulty in finding clients only looking for an excuse to part with money for wedding presents, first communion mementoes, or corporate gifts. One came to—and still comes to—Les Caves Augé for the very finest wines, the best vintages, the chateaus that defy all attempts at categorization, and they are all here: Latour, Haut Brion, Margaux, Romanée Conti, Yquem. With its solid brass ladder, enclosed cash desk, and dark wood shelves, Les Caves Augé resembles nothing more than one of the reading rooms at the National Library, the precious bottles lying in lieu of the weighty tomes that patiently await some erudite scholar to come and leaf through them. Even if Les

LES CAVES AUGÉ

Les Caves Augé on boulevard Haussman, not far from the church of Saint-Augustin, is like a cathedral to wine: the grand crus *are presented on the main altar, the lesser wines in the side chapels.*

LES CAVES AUGÉ

*The interior of Les Caves
Augé hasn't changed since 1850.
And it still has the same aim:
to provide the very best
of what France's wine
producers have to offer.*

Caves Augé were nothing other than a repository for these surefire wines, for many it would be worth a visit in its own right, but that alone is not enough to solicit the interest of the true amateurs who are motivated by a desire to share with others their passion for wine in the atmosphere that is so specific to Les Caves Augé. Their passion is not for the establishment wines but for the "dissident" wines, wines that are in some way different. For the past 16 years, Marc Sibard has been the Paris ambassador for these wines and the winemakers who produce them. He represents real winemakers who work their own vines without weeding everything around them, who only use the natural yeasts on the grapes for fermentation and let that fermentation occur naturally, without resorting to heating up the must so as to make it go faster; real winemakers who do not filter or remove the impurities artificially from their wine and use a minimum of sulfur, if they use it at all. And their wines have to be good, because Marc Sibard is unforgiving when it comes to taste. Ask him, and he is happy to give you his list of favorite winemakers, the ones who take risks, whose wines, as he puts it, are not afraid to reveal all: Thierry Cuzelet of Clos Tuboeuf in Cheverny, René Mosse in Anjou, Jérôme Prévost at Gueux in Champagne, Romaneaux Destezet in Saint Joseph, Bruno Duchêne in Collioure. These producers are only known now to a small cohort interested in these matters, but they are destined to be the great names of tomorrow. In promoting them now, Marc Sibard is continuing a long-established tradition at Les Caves Augé, that of stocking only the very best, regardless of the label. In any case, Sibard believes that a label is only worth the value he puts on it, rather like the art critic who determines the worth of a particular artist. Induction into this inner circle of Les Caves Augé—the outer circle is composed of those who come only for what is on the label—is akin to being welcomed into a religion, and Les Caves Augé has attracted a following among amateurs looking to share in the discovery of these new growers that for them are the way, the truth, and the light when it comes to wine. Which is somewhat of a pity, because it would be nice if Les Caves Augé could serve as a sort of school for everyone who wants to use their senses of taste and smell to buy "good" wine rather than just wines that stand out by virtue of their label.

Doubtless because he was aware of how closed this circle was, Marc Sibard agreed to become involved in opening Lavinia in Paris. Lavinia is somewhat of a UFO in the rarefied world of Paris wine merchants. Just a few paces from the Madeleine, its 16,000 square feet (1,500 square meters) spread over three floors is kept at a constant 66°F (19°C) and 70 percent humidity.

Thierry Servant, former head of L'Oréal in Spain, and his business associate Pascal Chevrot, businessmen and wine lovers both, had first tested the concept of a supermarket devoted to wine in

LAVINIA

Just round the corner from the Madeleine and spread over three floors, Lavinia has over six thousand different wines on offer from around the world. In the basement you can hunt down the finest vintages of the greatest wines in a temperature-controlled environment, and also find a wide selection of untreated wines.

Barcelona, but to do the same in the heart of conservative Paris was to gamble for even greater stakes. Not only were they launching the largest wine shop in Paris, but of the 6,500 different references they had in stock, 2,000 were from outside France, a death-defying risk in a city not noted for its tolerance of non-native wines. The whole of the ground floor is devoted to them: Château Musar from Lebanon, Sassicaïa from Chianti, "little" wines from Chile and even rare sparkling Chardonnays from England.

True wine lovers will be drawn to the basement, where most of the French and rare wines are to be found. In a cellar maintained at a constant 57°F (14°C), bottles of every vintage of Chateau Latour, Jaboulet Hermitage, or Amarone Bertoni are lined up imposingly. But there are also the wines made with little or no sulfur so dear to Marc Sibard, and that are made available here to the 8,500 members of the club that is the backbone of Lavinia's clientele. The ritual surrounding wine that is such an important—and imposing—aspect of Les Caves Augé is absent in this modern and functional space where the connoisseur and the debutant are put on an equal footing. Fact sheets, special signs denoting "Wines for under 10 euros," "Sommelier's Choice," and "Organic Wines" make buying wine less of a ritual and opens it up, if not to all comers, at least to all those who are interested. Paradoxically though, it is the connoisseurs who are likely to be most ecstatic about what they find here. Many years ago, the French chain Fnac was the first to sell books and music in the same way as others sold clothes; Lavinia hopes to do the same for Parisians when it comes to wine.

For those who remain immune to this type of merchandising, Paris is filled with local wine shops where buying wine remains a personal affair and the wine merchant if not a personal friend, is at least a willing accomplice. Les Caves Legrand is a good example of the sort of place where Parisians—who for the most part do not have their own cellars—nonetheless have the impression that their own personal reserve of fine wine is ageing nicely in the boutique's cellar. Since 1880 this venerable, not to say patrician, institution situated between the Galerie Vivienne and rue de la Banque has been to Paris what Berry Bros. & Rudd is to London, the arbiter of good taste when it comes to wine. Generations of Parisians have shopped here, not just for wine but also for fine foods and sweets. The boutique has retained the aura of an Ali Baba's cave about it, with its jars of hard candy, boxes of tea, and baskets of duck sausage. But above all one comes here for the wine. Legrand has always known how to change with the times. Until the end of the 1990s it was still being run by descendents of the founders, first by Lucien Legrand and then by his daughter Francine. Lucien Legrand was one of the

LAVINIA

At the Lavinia restaurant the wine is the same price as in the boutique. Chose your bottle off the shelf and drink it with your meal. Lavinia has democratized how wine is drunk in Paris. Women in particular enjoy this practical approach to wine.

LEGRAND

Weekly tasting sessions are organized around the U-shaped bar at Legrand.

first Paris wine merchants to hunt down the "little" winemakers who made and bottled their own wine, something which was not as common forty years ago as it is now. Parisians can thank him for the discovery of *domaines* that were relatively unknown at the time but that have since entered the pantheon, such as Zind Humbrecht in Alsace and La Grange des Pères in Languedoc. Despite being bought out by a wine dealer, the current team has maintained this tradition and come up with its own discoveries: Domaine Bizot in Vosne Romanée and the Rectorie in the Roussillon are just two of them. Legrand has also known how to adapt to the changing tastes of its Parisian clientele: on the Galerie Vivienne side a tasting area, complete with U-shaped bar and a *table d'hôte* menu, is the perfect setting to explore this newfound attitude to all things related to wine. Merchant banks are delighted to invite their clients for tastings of the most prestigious wines here, private individuals to celebrate a birthday or wedding with friends. Every Tuesday, wine experts and sommeliers host tastings for the uninitiated and soon Legrand is to make the cellars running underneath the arcade—with their thirty thousand bottles of France's finest wines (though this is only a fraction of the hundred thousand bottles or so that constitutes Legrand's war chest)—available for receptions in a truly remarkable setting. Legrand has mastered the art of seducing its customers.

In the same way as there are certain bookshops specializing in rare books, lovers of vintage wines can often find what they are looking for by rummaging through the collections belonging to certain dealers in antique wines. De Vinis Illustribus was started in 1994 by Lionel Michelin, a telecoms expert with a passion for old wines. When he first started, the location was secret, accessible only to those lucky enough to be accepted into the club, and even then by appointment only. It quickly became a pivotal operation in this highly specialized sector of the wine trade. He has recently opened a boutique for the general public, behind the Panthéon, housing an impressive collection of wines garnered from bankruptcy sales, successions, and remnants from the cellars of provincial wine merchants and restaurants being sold off. Collectors from around the world call him in search of a Cheval Blanc 1903 or a Romanée Conti 1937, but Lionel Michelin is just as happy to supply a missing Chambolle Musigny for a Paris amateur intent on having a bottle of every vintage in his collection, or provide a birthday gift for a loved one of a wine from the year they were born. Because there can be no doubting but that opening an old bottle of wine generates a very special set of emotions.

The wine trade is particularly keen on inner circles and brotherhoods. The history of Le Repaire de Bacchus is a case in point. Its founder, Dominique Fenouil, started life as a middle manager with

Philips, and in 1983 his employer gave him the not unpleasant task of buying five thousand cases of *Grands Crus Classés* to use as rewards in an incentive campaign for the sales force of one of its subsidiaries. The club that he created as part of this operation gave rise to the first Paris outlet of Le Repaire de Bacchus on rue des Acacias in the seventeenth arrondissement. For the first time in Paris, free tastings were on offer, some of which have gone down in the club's annals: such as the assortment of Petrus '78, Romanée Conti '84, and Yquem '81 offered for tasting in 1987 or the tasting of five vintages from Mouton Rothschild in 1988 and the same again, only this time with Latour, in 1990. Since then, the number of outlets has grown exponentially. There are twenty-nine

shops now in Paris and its environs, twelve of which continue the club's tasting sessions. Le Repaire de Bacchus's strength lies in the loyalty it has succeeded in generating among a predominantly well-off clientele that is happy to trust it and go along with its recommendations. The club now has six thousand members, so it can no longer afford to be as generous with the wines it offers for tasting as it was in the 1980s. The selection of wines has broadened, and nowadays it is the discoveries and personal favorites that Dominique Fenouil and his team come up with that draw the crowds: the Château Beaucastel from the Frères Perrin in Chateauneuf du Pape, the Château Le Thil from Jean de Laitre in Pessac Léognan, the Domaine Sarda Malet by Jérôme Malet on the Côtes du Roussillon, and the Château Hostens Picant from Sainte-Foy de Bordeaux. Le Repaire de Bacchus has also used the goodwill associated with its name to launch a range of spirits that have not been colored, caramelized, or otherwise adulterated, which it sells under the brand-name "Natural Color." Five types of spirits—armagnac, calvados, cognac, rum, and whiskey—are rolled out in thirty-three separate products, all contained in clear glass bottles so as best to display the lightness of the alcohol inside. Dominique Fenouil's revolution in this regard is all the more remarkable when one considers that—with the exception of J&B and Cutty Sark—practically all whiskey is artificially "darkened" and then bottled in opaque bottles so as to boost our impression of the spirit's strength. Interestingly, Paris has become the European test market for single malt whiskeys with distillers launching there for the first time specialties like vintage malts, whiskey that has been aged in oak barrels previously used for *grand cru* wines, and even whiskey straight from the barrel before it has had time to reduce. Boutiques like La Maison du Whisky now specialize in these limited edition whiskeys.

LEGRAND

Legrand near to place des Victoires has an amazing range of candies (see page 160) displayed side by side with grands crus *and table wines.*

Paris

on the go

Small snacks

LE BAR À SOUPES
*Red (gazpacho), yellow
(pumpkin), or green
(watercress)—the choice of
soups at Le Bar à Soupes on
rue de Charonne near the
Bastille is as colorful and
varied as an artist's palette.*

The word "restaurant" was first used in 1765 to designate a tavern where "restorative" soups were sold. Over the entrance of a certain Monsieur Boulanger's café on rue des Poulies was the inscription, "*Venite ad me omnes qui stomacho laboratis, et ego restaurabo vos,*" which literally translates as "Come unto me all ye whose stomachs labor, and I will restore you"—a parody of the Gospels. As the Enlightenment was well under way by then, Boulanger managed to avoid attracting the wrath of the Church, but he did upset the caterers' guild, who contested his right to sell food. When he eventually won his case before parliament, he opened the very first restaurant, which proved to be the forerunner of today's soup bars. Others followed, including the renowned chief caterer to the Comte de Provence, Antoine Beauvilliers, who founded the first upscale restaurant, La Grande Taverne de Londres, in 1784. But let us return to the "soup bars" that became hugely popular in Paris during the nineteenth century, when they were known as "*bouillons*"—in honor of the bouillon, or stock, that provides the main ingredient in any good soup—and that remained popular until after

LE BAR À SOUPES

Le Bar à Soupes is popular with both regulars, crazy about Anne-Catherine Bley's soup recipes, and tourists from the four corners of the world.

World War II because of their reasonable prices. Establishments like Chartier and Café du Commerce catered to thousands of workers every day. At the time, soup was a dish for the poor. With the advent of self-service restaurants and office cafeterias, the *bouillons* gradually disappeared. Like traditional restaurants, "soup bars" were a Parisian invention. But while the former thrived and went on to become a worldwide phenomenon, the latter owe their resurgence to influences from outside France and in particular to a phenomenon that originated in the United States. During the 1980s, soup—despite its rural connotations—began to crop up on the menus of U.S. city restaurants. The combination of good old-fashioned soup with the convenience of fast food owes its success primarily to women. In Paris, the first new-style "soup bar" opened in 2000, fueled by the success of the concept from the other side of the Atlantic. But in reality, owner Anne-Catherine Bley is perpetuating a time-honored Paris tradition in her premises, whose façade is New York cab yellow, on rue de Charonne just two minutes from the Bastille.

A former music industry marketing executive, she used none of her training when it came to launching her Bar à Soupes—she did it completely on instinct, and out of frustration at not being able to get a healthy, tasty, and natural meal next to where she worked. And what could be healthier, tastier, or more natural than soup? But unlike her counterparts in New York or Boston, she has opted for a huge choice of soups—over eighty in all—and the charm of her little establishment lies in the wide variety on offer. Of course, gazpacho makes its appearance in summer and vegetable soup in winter, but the winter menu also features—just to cite a few examples—split-pea soup with bacon, and tomato and apple soup with ricotta, and the summer menu includes carrot soup with coconut milk and meatball soup flavored with cumin seed.

Bley has refrained from opening other outlets and personally supervises the output of her chef Fritz Talvin, a former pastry chef also responsible for the traditional deserts that round out the menu, including homemade *clafoutis* and French-style crumble. The welcome is distinctly personal with Bley behind the cash register playing the role of big sister to her customers, never afraid to hand out advice ("That's enough protein") encouragement for those on a diet ("You've lost weight since the last time you were here") or just a warm word ("Enjoy today's selection of colors and flavors"). She even has something to say to the Japanese who have flocked to the Bar à Soupes ever since she appeared on Japanese public television channel NHK: "*Arigato!*" The soup bar on rue de Charonne has become something of an institution, a slice of gastronomic life as it were in

SOUPES
DE SAISON

Uniquement des ingrédients naturels prép
comme à la maison par le chef Giraudet. Le
de soupes varie en fonction des saisons,
les grands classiques et des saveurs à déco
Le chef vous suggère d'accompagner cert
recettes de soupe d'une quenelle aux cér
pochée Giraudet.

one of Paris's hippest neighborhoods, where Bley, far from trying to start a franchise empire, is quietly working away at her own version of a restaurant where everything is "handmade" and the soups are haute cuisine.

At the same time Anne-Catherine Bley was launching her operation near the Bastille, Giraudet, which for over a hundred years has been producing and distributing traditional soups, was looking to capitalize on its experience by opening its first retail outlet. Since 2002, the designer Bar à Soupes et Quenelles has been doing just that a few yards from the Marché Saint-Germain. It is a roaring success with the publishers and bourgeois bohemians who populate Paris's sixth arrondissement— it would be all the more surprising if Bley hadn't already demonstrated that soup has come a long way from its populist roots to become one of the favorite dishes of a certain elite. Even more unusual is how the same people have taken to the traditional quenelle from the Bresse region, simply poached and served as an accompaniment to soup or as part of a series of *tapas à la bressane*— evidence of a return to the gastronomic values of a past century. The quenelle has long been a staple of Lyonnais cooking. It was considered the ultimate delicacy, whether made from pike, chicken, or crayfish. Giraudet's Michel Porfiro prefers to use semolina or rye instead of flour or breadcrumbs in his quenelles to keep them as light as possible. A few yards from the restaurant, on rue Mabillon, Giraudet has opened a boutique where the full range of Porifiro's specialties is on sale. Nowhere else in Paris can you find such a selection of miniature culinary masterpieces—quenelles of pike or crayfish, with morels or porcini, with rye and hazelnut oil, or simply plain with sesame oil—as well as an organic range. Handmade quenelles line the immaculate store window like so many jewels waiting to be chosen by discerning gourmets.

**BAR À SOUPES
ET QUENELLES**

The design of the Bar à Soupes et Quenelles, near the Marché Saint-Germain, is resolutely modern and it attracts a loyal following at lunchtime from the artists, publishers, and journalists that populate the neighborhood. Favorite soups can also be taken out in bottles.

LA CRÉMERIE

LA CRÉMERIE

*In the Odéon district,
La Crémerie has succeeded
in combining the dual role
of first-class charcuterie
and wine bar, and also
manages to be one of the
most charming spots in the
area. The Barkel slicing
machine purrs quietly while
customers drink in a delightful
turn-of-the-century interior.*

While Paris is increasingly taken with a simpler and faster approach to food, there is still a preoccupation with quality, tradition, and authenticity. All three are in evidence at La Crémerie, also known as the Caves Miard, just a few yards from Odéon. The old-fashioned interior of this tiny space has been preserved, including a beautiful ceiling under glass. But instead of cheeses and cream from Normandy, La Crémerie offers a selection of the finest Italian cold cuts and has a cellar with some magnificent French wines. While owner Pierre Jancou may not be officially affiliated with the Slow Food association that works to protect culinary traditions, he adheres resolutely to its spirit. One comes to La Crémerie to enjoy *culatello di zibello*, the hind quarters of a pig aged for two years in a cellar; *coppa*; *spalla cruda di Piacenza*; or the stunning *lardo* from Colonnata in Tuscany, which is soaked in a brine flavored with cloves, cinnamon, rosemary, green peppercorns, and sea salt, and aged in Carrara marble cellars. Or try the organic Parmesan made by Signor Panini, "for the fun of it," and aged for almost three years on his 740-acre (300-hectare) estate. In the middle of La Crémerie lies the Rolls Royce of slicers, a 1930s Barkel that has been lovingly restored by Italian craftsmen. The Dutch firm Barkel stopped producing this type of machine in the 1950s, but the Italians have continued to maintain their fleet. Jancou is the Paris representative of this long tradition. He also stocks a wide selection of delicacies from Italy: *mostarda di frutta* from Cremona; balsamic vinegar from Reggio and Cremona, and its byproduct, *fragolaceto* jam made from whole strawberries marinated in the vinegar; and, of course, olive oils from Tuscany and Sicily. Everything is available either to eat in the store or take home. Chances are that once you have done the former, you will want to do the latter. And, if you wish to take an "Italian" tour of Paris, Pierre Jancou is your man: he willingly shares his list of favorite Italian trattorias in the city. And if Jancou sends you, red carpets will unroll to welcome you. La Crémerie may be small, but it is certainly perfectly formed.

LA CRÉMERIE

La Crémerie, a former bar since converted into a table d'hôte restaurant, has a wealth of surprises to discover, including Italian cold meats, organic wines carefully selected by Pierre Jancou, and delicious preserved tomatoes and peppers sprinkled with the finest olive oil.

British by birth but French by adoption, the humble sandwich has long been a staple of the traditional French brasserie. Whether made from a crusty baguette or—a more recent trend—from whole-wheat bread, it is under assault from Italian *panini*, American hamburgers, Japanese sushi, and Chinese dim sum. The brunt of this assault is borne by café owners whose quick and simple dishes, such as the *croque monsieur*, fed generations of workers anxious to grab a quick bite during their lunch break. Mass-produced sandwiches sought to fill a gap in the market, but they suffer from the same deficiencies as the "foreign" competition, namely ingredients that are not of the best quality, a tendency to aim for the lowest common denominator, and a combination of quantity with

speed rather than speed with quality. So when Alain Cojean and Fréderic Maquair offered both speed and quality at the first Cojean restaurant, which opened near the Madeleine in 2001, heads began to turn. They had a simple objective: feed as many people as possible, in as short a space of time as feasible, with dishes that could be eaten on the premises or brought back to the office. So far, normal. Where their concept differs is their insistence on the quality of the raw materials and the importance of genuinely fresh-tasting food, in contrast to previous approaches that involved using frozen foods and a "dumbing down" of flavors. And it is not just Cojean's predominantly blue décor that contributes to the sense of freshness. The cellophane-wrapped sandwiches are made fresh each morning; the fruit juice is squeezed on the premises; the wraps and daily specials are made fresh in the on-site kitchen. A delicious herb salad combines cilantro, chervil, chives, basil, arugula, Webb lettuce, and spinach, while the "self-tanning" salad combines freshly grated carrot with orange juice and cinnamon. Both are evidence of the obsession with freshness. Cojean and Maquair chose Bermudes, reputed to be the finest purveyor of fresh herbs at the Rungis market south of Paris, to supply them with vegetables. Standards are equally high in other areas with suppliers delivering fresh produce direct from Rungis to the different outlets each morning, perpetuating a time-honored tradition, albeit in a resolutely modern surrounding. And what is the secret of its success? There is no secret! Everything is right there to be seen on the plate in front of you: hard work, imagination, and a thorough respect for the customer explain why Cojean is the most talked about fast-food concept in Paris at the moment.

COJEAN

If you are wondering where to go for a quick, healthy meal in the busy heart of the Madeleine, try Cojean. Above is the latest outlet on boulevard Haussmann. Following pages: Two photographs show how the "feminine touch" interior has helped to convert Parisians to the joys of snacking.

DELICABAR

*In the heart of the Bon Marché,
in a strictly Pop Art ambience,
the Delicabar provides a staging
post for fashion victims in need
of a break, with its choice of
"bubbles" (carrot, for example)
and fruit jellies.*

Fashion is such an important aspect of the Delicabar that it is situated not just in the Bon Marché, the chic Left Bank department store, but on the same floor as ladies' fashions. It is as if to underline the fact that stylishness and *gourmandise* go hand in hand. Or is it that one complements the other? Whichever, after a busy half day's shopping, the average Parisienne could do with a little something light to round off the pleasure, much in the same way as elegant ladies in bygone times sought indulgences after committing venial sins. For those afraid of putting on weight, Sébastien Gaudard, formerly head chef at Fauchon, has concocted intensely flavored delicacies that weigh lightly on the stomach. His "bubbles," shortbread pastry topped with a feather-light mousse and infused with aromas of fruit and vegetables, come in exotic carrot or mango pulp versions, while chocolate is a more classical variant. Once again, sweet and savory go hand in hand. The *mille-feuille* and the sabayon, those classics of the pastry chef's repertory, both come in sweet and savory versions: the sabayon is made with chervil and zucchini, or with chocolate and citrus fruits; the *mille-feuille* is made with caramel and apple, or with a *confit* of vegetables and eggplant caviar. And in order to confuse you even further, there is pepper-flavored ganache in the chocolate cake. Gaudard, relishing his role as pastry chef turned cook, constantly innovates in his quest to change the way we think about food. In the colorful Pop Art interior, a huge display case doubles as a bar so customers can eat in or take out as they see fit. Which is only right, because a trip to the Delicabar is right at any time of the day: for a mid-morning or late-afternoon snack, for brunch as much as for lunch. Chances are that you will spot the brightly colored tartlets, but be sure not to miss the chocolate bars with their squares (or is it rectangles?) that come in three sizes: small, medium, and large, just like the clothes for sale nearby. The chocolate, hazelnut, or almond breakfast spreads come in tubes, like toothpaste—no doubt another

DELICABAR

*At the bar, the pastries
are all the more tempting
because they are right
in front of your eyes.
Irresistible.*

coded reference to beauty products. A final detail: the bags that Delicabar provides for carrying home the precious delicacies purchased. They are worn across the shoulder so as to avoid unsightly bags drooping from each arm—such details matter in the world of fashion.

No survey of the "best and freshest" would be complete without mentioning Pomze, the first boutique devoted entirely to apples and their by-products. Apples, along with grapes, are the most universal food there is, being both food and drink. At Pomze, you can be sure to find your favorite fruit in all its forms. Throughout the year, there are some sixty varieties of apple from around the world as well as a similar range of single-variety apple juices, thirty or so unpasteurized farmhouse ciders, and a selection of the finest Calvados and *pommeau* (an apple-based aperitif) together with some excellent perry. Pomze was launched by Daniel and Emmanuel Dayan, two globetrotters who cut their teeth with the Flo catering group in Tokyo. This highly original and utterly charming store doubles as a restaurant where apples make their appearance both as a garnish and as a dessert. Genuine *tartes Tatin*; macaroons with Manzana Verde, an alcohol spirit flavored with apples from the Basque region; or *cannelés* (little cakes that are a specialty of Bordeaux) doused in calvados are all guaranteed to raise your spirits without raising your cholesterol level.

POMZE

At Pomze on boulevard Haussmann, you can find fresh apples at any time of the year. If necessary, they are imported from southern Africa, Australia, or New Zealand. They also do lunch, and why not finish up with a delicious pomme d'amour *with white chocolate, wrapped in a dark chocolate coating, little glasses filled with* panacotta *and green Manzana apple, or "Ivory Towers"—a white chocolate cake filled with stewed apple and orange (above).*

The gourmet's notebook

There are literally thousands of exciting culinary addresses in Paris, and it was not possible to list all of them here. The authors have made a personal selection of their favorite locations, and while all are in Paris, many are also happy to deliver orders abroad.

SWEET PARIS

CONFECTIONERY AND CHOCOLATES

LES BONBONS
6, rue Bréa, 75006
Tel: +33 (0)1 43 26 21 15
This miniscule boutique in Montparnasse is well known for its huge choice of confectionery from all over France.

CHRISTIAN CONSTANT
37, rue d'Assas, 75006
Tel: +33 (0)1 53 63 15 15
E-mail: christianconstant@wanadoo.fr
This chocolate maker is one of the capital's true masters: try his orangettes made from Sicilian mandarins or his truffles and chocolate creams.

DEBAUVE ET GALLAIS
30, rue des Saints-Pères, 75007
Tel: +33 (0)1 45 48 54 67
> Other address:
   33, rue Vivienne, 75002
   Tel: +33 (0)1 40 39 05 50
This beautiful boutique in Saint-Germain-des-Prés has lots of original ideas like the pistoles Marie-Antoinette and little Arabica coffee beans coated in chocolate (keep a stock handy, just in case).

À L'ÉTOILE D'OR
30, rue Fontaine, 75009
Tel: +33 (0)1 48 74 59 55
(See photographs pp. 22–25)
A visit to this little boutique on place Pigalle is quite an experience. Denise Acabo will enchant you with her knowledge of France's confectionery. And only in her shop can you find such a selection of specialties from the country's best craftsmen, with chocolates from Bernachon in Lyon, Dufoux in Burgundy, and marshmallows from Nancy.

FOUQUET
22, rue François Iᵉʳ, 75008
Tel: +33 (0)1 47 23 30 36
www.fouquet.fr
E-mail:info@fouquet.fr
> Other address:

36, rue Laffitte, 75009
Tel: +33 (0)1 47 70 85 00)
This superb store has an excellent choice of confectionery, including fondants that are not so easy to find. They offer shipping world wide.

LE FURET
63, rue Chabrol, 75010
Tel: +33 (0)1 47 70 48 34
Fax: +33 (0)1 42 46 34 41
This first-class craftsman has chocolates and cakes, but also offers a range of traditional and original jams and jellies.

HÉDIARD
21, place de la Madeleine, 75008
Tel: +33 (0)1 43 12 88 88
> Four other addresses in Paris
A fine food store where everything is fabulous.

JEAN-PAUL HÉVIN
231, rue Saint-Honoré, 75001
(Boutique and tearoom)
Tel: +33 (0)1 55 35 35 96
www.jphevin.com
> Other addresses:
   3, rue Vavin, 75006
   Tel: +33 (0)1 43 54 09 85;
   23 bis, avenue de la Motte-Picquet, 75007
   Tel: +33 (0)1 45 51 77 48
(See photographs pp. 2, 4 [center], 12, 14–17)
Chocolates with cheese (Roquefort is our favorite) but also more traditional chocolates like the best-selling Carupana that mixes a ganache with three types of honey, miniature Florentine cookies, Paladins with pecan nuts, and candied chestnuts that are less sweet than the traditional marron glacé. In the cake line there is the Turin made from a mousse of candied chestnuts, the Safi flavored with orange, and the Guayaquil with either bitter chocolate or a combination of raspberry and chocolate. Also a range of dream gifts like the chocolate heart that resembles the finest lace, and the Kheops chocolates with marzipan and pistachio.

LA MAISON DU CHOCOLAT
225, rue du Faubourg-Saint-Honoré, 75008

Tel: +33 (0)1 42 27 39 44
www.lamaisonduchocolat.com
> Other addresses:
   19, rue de Sèvres, 75006
   Tel: +33 (0)1 45 44 20 40;
   56, rue Pierre Charron, 75008
   Tel: +33 (0)1 47 23 38 25;
   8, boulevard de la Madeleine, 75009
   Tel: +33 (0)1 47 42 86 52
   89, avenue Raymond Poincaré, 75016
   Tel: +33 (0)1 40 67 77 83
(See photographs pp. 30–33)
Robert Linxe, Basque by birth, never ceases to amaze with his creations. Do not attempt to resist the Marroni with its unsweetened mousse of marrons glacés, or the Rigoletto —a light truffle mix combined with caramelized butter—the Zagora with fresh mint, the lemon-flavored Andalousie, or the chocolate prunes, not to mention his divine éclairs flavored with chocolate, coffee, or caramel.

PIERRE MARCOLINI
89, rue de Seine, 75006
Tel: +33 (0)1 44 07 39 07
www.marcolini.be
> Other address:
   Chez Flamant
   8, rue Furstemberg, 75006
   Tel: +33 (0)1 56 81 12 40
(See photographs pp. 11, 18–21)
In this ultramodern setting, the chocolate maker from Brussels has set Paris on fire with his "chocolate squares" and tea-flavored ganaches that include Earl Grey, jasmine, milk, and lemon varieties.

À LA MÈRE DE FAMILLE
35, rue du Faubourg Montmartre, 75009
Tel: +33 (0)1 47 70 83 69
(See photographs pp. 26–29)
A beautiful old setting—among the most famous in Paris—for this paradise on earth where chocolates from all over France will lead you into temptation. The problem is deciding what to choose.

À LA REINE ASTRID
16, rue du Cherche-Midi, 75006
Tel: +33 (0)1 42 84 07 02

> Other address:
   33, rue Washington, 75008
   Tel: +33 (0)1 45 63 60 39
A good chocolate shop, not far from the Bon Marché department store.

CAKES LARGE AND SMALL

ANGÉLINA
226, rue de Rivoli, 75001
Tel: +33 (0)1 42 60 82 00
A very pretty tearoom and patisserie with an interior which is listed as historically important. The Mont Blanc made from whipped cream and chestnut purée should not be missed.

LA BAGUE DE KENZA
106, rue Saint-Maur, 75011
Tel: +33 (0)1 43 14 93 15
> Other addresses:
   233, rue de la Convention, 75015;
   207, rue du Faubourg Saint-Antoine, 75010
(See photographs pp. 44–47)
The Algerian pastries that are piled high here are given a French touch that keeps them light and smooth.

BOISSIER CHOCOLATIER
184, avenue Victor Hugo, 75016
Tel: +33 (0)1 45 03 50 77
www.maison-boissier.com
The fruit-balls here are famous, but the chocolates and tearoom are also worth the trip.

LES CAKES DE BERTRAND
7, rue Bourdaloue, 75009
Tel: +33 (0)1 40 16 16 28
(See photographs pp. 38–43)
Located just behind the Notre-Dame de Lorette church, this pretty, old-fashioned tearoom has a plethora of tempting culinary gift ideas and a range of cakes—sweet and savory— that you can taste on the spot or take home.

LAURENT DUCHENE
2, rue Wurtz, 75013
Tel: +33 (0)1 45 65 00 77
E-mail: laurent.duchene@libertysurf.fr
In the heart of the thirteenth arrondissement this pastry shop is really worth a trip: delicious little almond cakes known as financiers,

and a host of other mouthwateringly moist tea-time cakes. The mini chocolate cakes that melt in the middle are a specialty. Incidentally, he is also one of the best bread bakers in Paris.

LA GRANDE ÉPICERIE DU BON MARCHÉ
26–38, rue de Sèvres, 75007
Tel: +33 (0)1 44 39 81 00
A huge choice of confectionery and cookies from around the world, together with wines, meat, fish, sandwiches, and salads are on offer here. A wide selection of foods that you can take home or eat in the store are on display next to a delicatessen counter that includes light and tasty daily specials.

PIERRE HERMÉ
72, rue Bonaparte, 75006
Tel: +33 (0)1 43 54 47 77
No guide to gourmet Paris can ignore this famous pastry chef.

LADURÉE
21, rue Bonaparte, 75006
Tel: +33 (0)1 44 07 64 87
www.laduree.fr
> Other addresses:
  16, rue Royale, 75008
  Tel: +33 (0)1 42 60 21 79;
  75, avenue des Champs-Élysées, 75008
  Tel: +33 (0)1 40 75 08 75
(See photographs pp. 48–51)
Three temples to the art of the macaroon, each with a nineteenth-century interior. Classics like raspberry, coffee, and rose are complemented by new inventions such as licorice and mint, with a new "collection" almost every season and a superb pastry shop with candy and chocolates of the highest quality that make excellent gifts.

PÂTISSERIE GÉRARD MULOT
76, rue de Seine, 75006
Tel: +33 (0)1 43 26 85 77
Excellent cakes that include a cherry pie (pick the plain version instead of the pistachio variety) and orange tart as well as first-class sandwiches and a wide choice

of rich and wholesome savory tarts, with salmon or vegetables, etc.

PÂTISSERIE VIENNOISE
8, rue de l'École de Médecine, 75006
Tel: +33 (0)1 43 26 60 48
Since 1928 this miniscule patisserie in the heart of the Latin Quarter has been a haunt for students, who come for its strudel, poppy-seed cakes, chocolates, and Viennese coffee.

SADAHARU AOKI
35, rue de Vaugirard, 75006
Tel: +33 (0)1 45 44 48 90
www.sadaharuaoki.com
> Other address:
  56, boulevard Port Royal 75005
  Tel: +33 (0)1 45 35 36 80
(See photographs pp. 34, 36–37)
Some of the specialties at this tiny boutique near the Luxembourg Gardens use green tea as a flavoring, but traditional French patisserie is also represented with a toffee tart that defies description!

LE STÜBLI
11, rue Poncelet, 75017
Tel: +33 (0)1 42 27 81 86
www.stubli.com
E-mail: stubli@club-internet.fr
Paris's German and Austrian pastry shop has apfelstrudel, black forest cake, sachertorte, linzertorte, and, at Christmas, shortbread cookies and zimsterne. A small restaurant on the first floor serves up German lunches. Treat yourself to a Viennese brunch on the weekend.

TEA AND COFFEE

LE CARRÉ DES SIMPLES
22, rue Tronchet, 75008
Tel: +33 (0)1 44 56 05 34
A pretty and modern boutique in the department store district with a selection of teas and essential oils, a choice of originally flavored herbal teas that include a children's brew, Colette flowers, and Lebanese white coffee.

COMPTOIRS RICHARD
48, rue du Cherche-Midi, 75006
Tel: +33 (0)1 42 22 45 93

www.richard.fr
> Other addresses:
  145, rue Saint-Dominique, 75007;
  10, rue La Fayette, 75009;
  73, rue Lecourbe, 75015;
  Tel: +33 (0)1 40 65 20 07;
  8, rue de Lévis, 75017
(See photographs pp. 68–73)
While coffee is the main attraction in these pretty boutiques, chocolates, biscuits, teas, and herbal teas are also on offer.

KILALI
3–5, rue des Quatre Vents, 75006
Tel: +33 (0)1 43 25 65 64
This boutique near the Marché Saint-Germain has recently opened and specializes in green teas. It also has its own tearoom hidden behind the blackened storefront.

LA MAISON DES TROIS THÉS
33, rue Gracieuse, 75005
Tel: +33 (0)1 43 36 93 84
www.maisondestroisthes.com
(See photographs pp. 58–63)
Possibly Paris's most mysterious shop. In a quiet back street behind the Panthéon is the world's largest tea shop. In an extraordinary design by the architect/designer François Muracciole there are no less than a thousand teas from Taiwan and China and vintage teas dating back to 1890.

MARIAGE FRÈRES
30–32, rue du Bourg-Tibourg, 75004
Tel: +33 (0)1 42 72 28 11
www.mariagefreres.com
> Other addresses:
  13, rue des Grands-Augustins, 75006
  Tel: +33 (0)1 40 51 82 50;
  260, rue du Faubourg-Saint-Honoré, 75008
  Tel: +33 (0)1 46 22 18 54)
(See photographs pp. 52, 54–57)
With its miniature tea museum, boutique, and tearoom, a visit to Mariage Frères is a real treat. Be sure to book for Sunday brunch, which is extremely popular.

LE PALAIS DES THÉS
61, rue du Cherche-Midi, 75006
Tel: +33 (0)1 42 22 03 98
> Other address:
  35, rue Abbé Grégoire, 75006
  Tel: +33 (0)1 45 48 85 81
A huge choice of teas, samovars, teapots, and a comprehensive library that is certain to satisfy any genuine tea lover.

CAFÉ VERLET
256, rue Saint-Honoré, 75001
Tel: +33 (0)1 42 60 67 39
(See photographs pp. 64–67)
Annual trips to the key coffee-producing regions of the world by this traditional coffee roaster ensure a stock of the very finest coffees. You can also order a cup while inhaling the aromas of the coffee being roasted on the premises.

ICE CREAM AND SORBET

Our list of the iced pleasures that the capital has to offer is by no means comprehensive, but no guide to gourmet Paris would be complete without a trip to the Île Saint-Louis or the banks of the Seine.

BERTHILLON
31, rue Saint-Louis-en-l'Île, 75004
Tel: +33 (0)1 43 54 31 61
www.berthillon-glacier.fr
Berthillon has been around for three generations and is world famous for its sorbets and ice creams. Do not be put off by the line outside the little boutique on rue Saint-Louis, the wait is worth it. Ice cream comes in a huge choice of flavors—coffee, whisky, fresh mint, caramel with ginger, and pine nut praline—but the macaroons filled with ice cream are doubly delicious.

DAMMANN'S
1, rue des Grands Degrés, 75006
Tel: +33 (0)1 43 29 15 10
Just a few steps from Notre-Dame, almost on the river bank, is a truly excellent ice cream shop—try their yogurt or unusual almond ice creams, available in cones or cups.

The gourmet's notebook

SAVORY PARIS

BREAD AND CHEESE

ANDROUËT
51, rue de Verneuil, 75007
Tel: +33 (0)1 45 48 51 98
www.androuet.com
Pierre Androuët was the first Paris cheese merchant to have given cheese its rightful place in the gastronomic landscape.

L'AUTRE BOULANGE
43, rue de Montreuil, 75011
Tel: +33 (0)1 43 72 86 04
(Closed on Saturday afternoons and Sundays)
Traditional and specialist breads as well as fougasses are on offer in this excellent address on the east side of Paris.

BARTHÉLEMY
51, rue de Grenelle, 75007
Tel: +33 (0)1 42 22 82 24
(See photographs pp. 94–97)
The cheese merchant that supplies the Faubourg Saint-Germain has a comprehensive choice of cheeses ripened to perfection by Monsieur and Madame Barthélemy.

BOULANGERIE KAYSER
85, boulevard Malesherbes, 75017
Tel: +33 (0)1 45 22 70 30
> Other addresses:
  8, rue Monge, 75005;
  10, rue de l'Ancienne Comédie, 75006;
  87, rue d'Assas, 75006;
  49, rue Linois, 75015;
  79, rue du Commerce, 75015
(See photograph pp. 86–89)
This is the most fashionable Parisian bakery of the moment with a huge selection of breads and four "collections" a year (one per season). The bread is always perfectly made thanks to the fermentolevain machine Éric Kayser invented so that every loaf has a fine crust and an impeccably formed crumb. The shops in the fifth and seventeenth arrondissements have a few tables for grabbing a quick snack.

BREAD & ROSES
7, rue de Fleurus, 75006
Tel: +33 (0)1 42 22 06 06
This new bakery next to the Luxembourg gardens has everything you need from hefty country loaves to organic bread with dried fruits and spelt bread as well as English brown bread, scones, muffins, a delicatessen counter, and a few tables for a quick snack.

MARIE ANNE CANTIN
12, rue du Champs de Mars, 75007
Tel: +33 (0)1 45 50 43 94
(See photographs pp. 98–99)
In a profession dominated by men, Marie-Anne Cantin stands out as a master cheese merchant. With her innate sense of hospitality she is a key player on the Paris food scene.

À LA FLÛTE GANA
226, rue des Pyrénées, 75020
Tel: +33 (0)1 43 58 42 62
Isabelle and Valérie Ganachaud are two of the best-known female bakers in France and their reputation has spread far beyond their Belleville neighborhood.

AU LEVAIN DU MARAIS
32, rue de Turenne, 75003
Tel: +33 (0)1 42 78 07 31
> Other addresses:
  28, boulevard Beaumarchais, 75011
  Tel: +33 (0)1 48 05 17 14;
  142, avenue Parmentier, 75011
  Tel: +33 (0)1 43 57 36 91
As in all the best boutiques you have to line up to be served bread here. People come from far and wide to enjoy the breads made with a natural leavening agent, the fougasses, and breakfast pastries.

MOISAN
5, place d'Aligre, 75012
Tel: +33 (0)1 43 45 46 60
> Other addresses:
  114, rue Paty, 75013
  Tel: +33 (0)1 45 83 08 13;
  4, avenue du Général Leclerc, 75014
  Tel: +33 (0)1 43 22 34 13;
  57, rue Fondary, 75015
  Tel: +33 (0)1 45 75 34 85
The best in organic bread, it is also available in some Monoprix stores.

LE MOULIN DE LA VIERGE
166, avenue de Suffren, 75015;
105, rue Vercingétorix, 75014
Tel: +33 (0)1 47 43 45 55
> Other address: 82, rue Daguerre, 75014
(See photographs pp. 4 left, 80–85)
Breads here are made with organic flour, baked in the old-fashioned way, and sold in old-fashioned authentic bakeries for local residents.

PAUL
33, rue Tronchet, 75008
(Protected façade)
Tel: +33 (0)1 40 17 99 54
www.paul.fr
> Several addresses including:
  25, avenue de l'Opéra, 75001
  Tel: +33 (0)1 42 60 78 22;
  77, rue de Seine, 75006
  Tel: +33 (0)1 55 42 02 23
(See photographs pp. 6, 90–93)
The marketing here is not overdone, and the bread is made according to traditional methods.

POILÂNE
8, rue Cherche-midi, 75006
Tel: +33 (0)1 45 48 42 59
www.poilane.com
Email for overseas orders:
info@poilane.fr
(See photographs pp. 76, 78–79)
No need to introduce Poilâne's bread, but the bakery on rue du Cherche-Midi is also a bread museum that includes an extraordinary collection of still lifes with bread as their theme. You can visit all areas, from the shop itself to the baking area.

FINE FOOD STORES

ALLICANTE
L'Huilerie de Paris
26, boulevard Beaumarchais, 75011
Tel/Fax: +33 (0)1 43 55 13 02
www.allicante.com
E-mail: allicante@allicante.com
(See photographs pp. 5 right, 104–105)
Next to the Bastille this boutique has a selection of oils including grape-seed, walnut, hazelnut, olive, and argan as well as spicy and flavored varieties such as black

and white truffle or cep mushroom, together with the best vinegars and all the advice you need to use them to their best advantage.

L'AVANT-GOÛT CÔTÉ CELLIER
37, rue Bobillot, 75013
Tel: +33 (0)1 45 81 14 06
This tiny fine-food store belongs to the talented chef from the Avant-Goût restaurant opposite. As well as a range of foods and wine, dishes from the restaurant can be ordered to take out.

BELLOTA BELLOTA
18, rue Jean Nicot, 75007
Tel: +33 (0)1 53 59 96 96
> Other address: boutique near the Champs-Élysées:
  JABUGO IBERICO ET CO
  11, rue Clément Marot, 75008
  Tel: +33 (0)1 47 20 03 13
(See photograph pp. 108–109)
Specialists in Spanish cured hams —Jamón Ibérico. Each variety is displayed on plates with details of its origin and curing time along with a range of Spanish wines carefully selected by these experts in Spanish gastronomy.

BYZANCE
27, rue Yves-Kermen,
92100 Boulogne
Tel: +33 (0)1 46 09 02 28
The other main supplier of caviar in the capital, Byzance has recently added Spanish hams and wines to its range. Twice a year they organize tastings and the chance to discover new products.

LE COMPTOIR DE LA GASTRONOMIE
34, rue Montmartre, 75001
Tel: +33 (0)1 42 33 31 32
Fax: +33 (0)1 42 33 72 45
(See photographs pp. 8 and 118)
Situated in Les Halles, this boutique opens from 6 A.M. to 7 P.M. as it might have done when this area was the former market district of Paris. Foie gras, salmon, wines, spirits, and a delicious chocolate cake are on offer behind a beautiful façade dating from the nineteenth century. At lunchtime a few tables are available for lunch.

COMPTOIR DU SAUMON & CIE
60, rue François Miron, 75004
Tel: +33 (0)1 42 77 23 08
Fax: +33 (0)1 42 77 44 75
With their Nordic atmosphere,
these boutiques are popping up
all over Paris and around France.
Salmon from the Baltic, Ireland,
and Norway lies alongside smoked
shark, eel, and tuna, as well as
herrings, and the vodka and
aquavit which are essential
accompaniments!

DALLOYAU
101, rue du Faubourg Saint-Honoré,
75008
Tel: +33 (0)1 42 99 90 00
www.dalloyau.com
> Other addresses:
  2, place Edmond Rostand,
  75006 Paris
  Tel: +33 (0)1 43 29 31 10
  Fax: +33 (0)1 43 26 25 72;
  5, boulevard Beaumarchais, 75004;
  69, rue de la Convention, 75015;
  63, rue de Grenelle, 75007
A delicatessen with a history
that stretches back in time,
much to the delight of those
lucky enough to live close by.

DA ROSA
62, rue de Seine, 75006
Tel: +33 (0)1 40 51 00 09
Fax: +33 (0)1 40 51 04 59
www.darosa.fr
(Open every day from 10 A.M. to 10 P.M.)
(See photographs pp. 110–111)
A wonderful fine food store that
also has a few tables where you
can taste the products on display,
in particular real "Ibérico" ham.
A selection of specialty sweets
completes the choice on offer
—the raisins soaked in Sauternes
and dipped in chocolate are
a perfect accompaniment to
coffee and absolutely irresistible.

DAVOLI
34, rue Clerc, 75007
Tel: +33 (0)1 47 05 20 74
The best Italian delicatessen in
the chic seventh arrondissement
has a choice of wines, charcuterie
and take-out dishes: your guests
will love the vitello tonnato.

DUBERNET
2, rue Augereau, 75007
Tel: +33 (0)1 45 55 50 71
Everything you could want from
the southwest of France: foie gras,
preserved foods, pâtés, and hams
along with vacuum-packed cooked
dishes like veal stew and boiled
bacon.

FAUCHON
26, place de la Madeleine, 75008
Tel: +33 (0)1 47 42 60 11
www.fauchon.com
The grand old lady of place Madeleine,
the favorite fine food store of Paris's
upper crust is also a patisserie
and delicatessen, and offers snacks
and packed lunches produced by the
Flo group. They offer shipping world
wide.

LA FERMERIE
24, rue Surcouf, 75007
Tel: +33 (0)1 45 55 23 03
Fax: +33 (0)1 45 55 25 07
(Open Monday through Saturday from
10 A.M. to 2 P.M. and 4 P.M. to 9 P.M.)
Farm produce is on the menu at this
shop in the Champ de Mars district
including cheese, foie gras, hams,
and jams.

GOUMANYAT-ÉPICES
3, rue Dupuis, 75003
A secret address that no guide to
Paris's culinary delights can ignore.

GRANTERROIRS
30, rue Miromesnil, 75008
Tel: +33 (0)1 47 42 18 18
Delicacies from Provence and all over
the Mediterranean are the specialty
here. You can taste everything
beforehand at one of the tables
in the restaurant.

ITALIA
9, rue de Lévis, 75017
Tel: +33 (0)1 43 87 01 00
Fax: +33 (0)1 43 87 01 50
E-mail: pasta.nostrana@wanadoo.fr
The best Italian delicatessen on
this street devoted to the pleasures
of food. Pastas, of course, but also
wines and deserts. The miniature
babas and the limoncello are
unforgettable.

IZRAËL
30, rue François Miron, 75004
Tel: +33 (0)1 42 72 66 23
Fax: +33 (0)1 42 72 86 32
(See photographs pp. 4 right,
116–117)
You could be forgiven for thinking
you were in a bazaar in Morocco
or Istanbul when you step into
this boutique in the Marais.

LAFAYETTE GOURMET
40, boulevard Haussmann, 75009
Tel: +33 (0)1 42 82 34 56
A huge food hall with a selection
of goods from around the world
and also the Bellota Bellota stand
with its Spanish hams and Fatima
Hal's Moroccan salads, tagines,
and couscous.

LAFAYETTE MAISON
(Food counter)
35, boulevard Haussmann, 75009
In the brand new Lafayette Maison,
Sylvain Gaudu, who runs Lafayette
Gourmet's food halls, has launched
a food counter in the basement
that is well worth a visit, with a huge
choice of hams (the Portuguese
version is our favorite) and wines.

LEBLANC
6, rue Jacob, 75006
Tel: +33 (0)1 46 34 61 55
(See photograph pp. 106–107)
"Fruit" oils (walnut, hazelnut,
pine-nut, sesame, and colza)
are the specialty at this Paris
outlet of France's leading
traditional oil mill.

LENÔTRE
44, rue d'Auteuil, 75016
Tel: +33 (0)1 45 24 52 52
Fax: +33 (0)1 42 30 79 45
www.lenotre.fr/en
> Other address:
  15, boulevard de Courcelles, 75008
  Tel: +33 (0)1 45 63 87 63
  And several other addresses
  throughout the city
Gourmets remember with nostalgia
Gaston Lenôtre's unforgettable
cakes when he first set up shop
in Paris. While Lenôtre may since
have opened new outlets, the quality
has remained as high.

LA MAISON DE L'OLIVE
3, rue Ampère, 75017
Tel: +33 (0)1 47 66 55 13
Fax: +33 (0)1 47 66 55 14
Specialists in genuine olive oil
from small producers.

LA MAISON DU DANEMARK
Restaurant Flora Danica
142, avenue des Champs-Élysées,
75008
Tel: +33 (0)1 44 13 86 26
www.restaurantfloradanica.com
Two restaurants with Scandinavian
specialties and a boutique with a wide
selection of soused herrings, salmon,
and aquavit.

MAVROMATIS
47, rue Censier, 75005
Tel: +33 (0)1 45 35 96 50
Fax: +33 (0)1 43 36 13 08
The best Greek delicatessen in Paris
is to be found at the bottom of rue
Mouffetard. The city's Greek
population comes here for its retsina,
taramasalata, and tzatziki.

À L'OLIVIER
23, rue de Rivoli, 75004
Tel: +33 (0)1 48 04 86 59
For many years Paris's only specialist
in quality olive and other oils
and their by-products.

OLIVIERS & CO
8, rue de Lévis, 75017
Tel: +33 (0)1 53 42 18 04
(See photographs pp. 100, 102–103)
A chain of stores primarily dedicated
to olive oil: a wide selection and
a constant attention to quality and
information on the oils on display.
This is the only outlet where you can
eat, at a long table shared with other
diners, but Oliviers and Co boutiques
are found in all the best gourmet
shopping streets in Paris including
the rue de Buci, rue Vieille-du-Temple,
and Bercy.

PETROSSIAN
18, boulevard de la Tour Maubourg,
75007
Tel: +33 (0)1 44 11 32 22
Fax: +33 (0)1 44 11 32 25
www.petrossian.fr/www.petrossian.com
(See photographs pp. 112–113)

The gourmet's notebook

No surprise that you can find the very best caviar here (the Imperial is our favorite), but also smoked wild salmon, cod with dill, or à la caucasienne, *Pacific salmon roe as well as a variety of smoked fish such as sturgeon, eel, and herring. But Petrossian also has a range of fine foods like borscht, or chocolate drops with vodka and a small dining area where you can have a plate of smoked fish accompanied by a glass of wine or vodka (plain, cherry, or herb flavored), or a crab or salmon sandwich to take out. They offer shipping world wide.*

AUX PIPALLOTTES GOURMANDES
49, rue Rochechouart, 75009
Tel: +33 (0)1 44 53 04 53
(See photograph p. 119)
The few brightly colored tables at this delicatessen on the way to Montmartre are besieged at lunchtime. Open every day, it offers a selection of the most exciting foods on sale in the store (chutneys, pâtés, preserved foods), and biscuits, cakes, pastries (such as "grandmother's" chocolate cake) and desserts like the chocolate crème brulée, and teas from Mariage Frères. It also has a range of fruit- and vegetable-based cosmetics like cucumber cold cream and peach body scrub.

AU RÉGAL
4, rue Nicolo, 75016
Tel: +33 (0)1 42 88 49 15
Russian specialties at this superb 1930s store include salmon and smoked sturgeon, pierogi (little pastry appetizers), and—with advance notice— the best koulibiac in Paris.

SUR LES QUAIS
7, place d'Aligre, 75012
Tel: +33 (0)1 43 43 21 09
In the covered market at place d'Aligre you can find an interesting selection of olive oils and spices.

ROSE BAKERY
46, rue des Martyrs, 75009
Tel: +33 (0)1 42 88 12 80
Undoubtedly one of the best brunches in Paris is to be found here, but this is also a fine food store specializing in English and American delicacies such as maple syrup from Vermont, organic fruit juices from Devon, cheese from the celebrated Neal's Yard Dairy in London, organic bries, carrot cake, brownies, cheese cakes, and scones. Bread and butter is placed on the table on arrival and there are teas of all hues —black, green or red from South Africa—and organic beer or wine. Ask for Rose or Jean-Charles.

TANG FRERES
48, avenue d'Ivry, 75013
Tel: +33 (0)1 45 70 80 00
Fax: +33 (0)1 53 61 16 03
> Other address:
   168, avenue de Choisy, 75013
   Tel: +33 (0)1 44 24 06 72
The capital's best Asian grocery has everything from ginger to woks, from dried noodles to exotic fruits and coriander. All one needs to become a master of the Far East.

TERRES DE TRUFFES
21, rue Vignon, 75008
Tel: +33 (0)1 53 43 80 44
(See photographs pp. 114–115)
Next to the Madeleine, this pretty and new boutique was opened by a chef originally from the South of France, Bruno de Lorges. Truffles are the stars of course, but their derivatives play a strong supporting role—truffled cheese and truffled ice cream to name but two. The minimalist dining room is perfect for tasting the wares on display, but you can also order dishes to take out or buy some tortellini with truffles to cook at home.

TREO
112, rue des Dames, 75017
Tel: +33 (0)1 44 69 94 00
Parmesan, Parma ham, and white truffles (when they are in season) are all served here in a décor and with an attention to detail that is second to none.

PARIS IN A GLASS

AUGÉ
116, boulevard Haussmann, 75008
Tel: +33 (0)1 45 22 16 97
(See photographs pp. 126–129)
This is an absolute must, as much for the great names in wine, as for the "natural" wines and the superb advice that is dispensed in an interior that has remained unchanged since the Second Empire, all of which has made it a veritable temple for genuine wine lovers.

LE BARON ROUGE
1, rue Théophile Roussel, 75012
Tel: +33 (0)1 43 43 14 32
Alongside the Aligre market, the patrons of this wine shop are so numerous they end up spilling onto the sidewalk.

CAVES TAILLEVENT
199, rue du Faubourg Saint-Honoré, 75008
Tel: +33 (0)1 45 61 14 09
The Michelin three-star restaurant's boutique has one of the best selections of Burgundies in Paris.

COLETTE
213, rue Saint-Honoré, 75001
Tel: +33 (0)1 55 35 33 90
Fax: +33 (0)1 55 35 33 99
www.colette.fr
Choose a glass of water from the dozens on offer to accompany a quick snack at the bar or at one of the tables in the basement.

LA DERNIÈRE GOUTTE
6, rue Bourbon-le-Château, 75006
Tel: +33 (0)1 43 29 11 62
(Open from 10 A.M. to 8:30 P.M.; Sunday from 11 A.M. to 7 P.M. and Monday from 4 P.M. to 8:30 P.M.)
(See photographs pp. 121–122, 124–125)
This wine shop is run by a young American wine lover who is particularly keen on wines from the Languedoc and has made it his business to introduce them to Paris.

L'ÉCLUSE
15, quai des Grands Augustins, 75006
Tel: +33 (0)1 46 33 58 74
www.leclusebaravin.com
(Six locations in Paris: Bastille, Champs-Élysées, Madeleine and a wine shop at 1, rue d'Amaillé, 75017)

A concentration of Bordeaux wines and a few regional dishes or a foie gras with a glass of Sauternes and a legendary chocolate cake make up the menu and give a homey touch to what was one of the first wine bars in Paris.

IDEA VINO
88, avenue Parmentier, 75011 Paris
Tel: +33 (0)1 43 57 10 34
Fax: +33 (0)1 43 57 10 73
Supplier to all the best Italian restaurants. Its Barolos and Chiantis are particularly noteworthy as is the Modena mustard and the organic risotto made with squid ink or cepes.

LAVINIA
3–5, boulevard de la Madeleine, 75001
Tel: +33 (0)1 42 97 20 24
www.lavinia.fr
E-mail: laviniafrance@lavinia.fr
(See photographs pp. 130–133)
This is not a supermarket, more like a wine department store with seven thousand types and the widest choice of foreign wines in Paris.

LEGRAND FILLES ET FILS
1 rue de la Banque, 75002
Tel: +33 (0)1 42 60 07 12
www.caves-legrand.com
> Other address:
   119, rue du Dessous-des-Berges, 75013
   Tel: +33 (0)1 45 83 85 88
(See photographs pp. 5, 134–137, 160)
A stone's throw from place des Victoires, with a magnificent old-fashioned décor that leads to the Galerie Vivienne, Legrand is famous for its wine but also offers a selection of confectionary and traditional sweets.

LA MAISON DU WHISKY
20, rue d'Anjou, 75008
Tel: +33 (0)1 47 30 71 90
Fax: +33 (0)1 47 30 71 91
www.whisky.fr
This is a temple in honor of whiskey: with its single malts, "limited editions," undiluted whiskey "straight from the cask," and other "collector's items," it is full of whiskeys that are hard to find, even in Scotland.

LE REPAIRE DE BACCHUS
88, rue de Montorgueil, 75002
Tel/Fax: +33 (0)1 42 36 17 49
*Twenty-eight outlets in Paris
with a good selection of wines
and spirits and a particularly
interesting range of spirits sold
under the name "natural color"
that includes Armagnac, cognac,
and whisky that have been aged
naturally and without added color.*

DE VINIS ILLUSTRIBUS
2, rue des Lyonnais, 75005
Tel: +33 (0)1 43 36 12 12
Fax: +33 (0)1 43 36 20 30
www.devinis.fr
(Open Monday through Saturday from
11 A.M. to 8 P.M.)
*With its wines for special occasions,
this specialist offers tasting evenings
in the cellar and dispatches orders
around France and abroad.*

PARIS ON THE GO

LE BAR À SOUPES
33, rue de Charonne, 75011
Tel: +33 (0)1 43 57 53 79
www.lebarasoupes.com
E-mail: info@lebarasoupes.com
(See photographs pp. 140,
142–143)
*Anne-Catherine Bley's little
yellow boutique is just next
to the Bastille, and she has recently
written a book of soup recipes.
Every day there is a soup of
the day and a choice of five
other seasonal soups. Our
favorites are pea and mint,
nettle, and pumpkin with cinnamon.
You can take out or eat in.*

BAR À SOUPES ET QUENELLES
5, rue Princesse, 75006
Tel: +33 (0)1 43 25 44 44
Fax: +33 (0)1 43 25 07 87
www.giraudet.fr
(See photographs pp. 144–145)
> Other address: 16, rue Mabillon,
  75006
*Soups here come in little bottles that are
perfect for two people, or if you prefer
you can have a bowl on the premises.
In winter, our favorite is chestnut and
lentil, and in spring it is a toss up
between asparagus, pea, or broad
bean. Giraudet, the originator of these
creations, also specialises in dumplings.*

BE
73, boulevard de Courcelles, 75008
Tel: +33 (0)1 46 22 20 20
(Open Monday through Saturday 8 A.M.
to 9 P.M.)
*The partnership between Alain
Ducasse and Eric Kayser has
produced this combination of breads,
sandwiches, soups, and salads
(from the baker) and fine foods
(from Ducasse) like tins of first-class
tuna straight from Bilbao, Italian olive
oil, wonderful antico balsamic vinegar,
as well as risottos and handmade pasta.*

COJEAN
17, boulevard Haussmann, 75009
Tel: +33 (0)1 47 70 22 65
Fax: +33 (0)1 47 70 22 68
> Other addresses:
  6, rue de Sèze, 75009;
  19, rue de la Monnaie, 75001
(See photographs pp. 5, 139, 150–153)
*A few steps from Galeries Lafayette
on the corner of rue du Helder,
in an ultramodern American style
interior, you can find delicious soups*

*and the freshest salads (like a Caesar
salad) adorned with herbs guaranteed
to be packed with vitamins. Fresh
sandwiches—with crab, with herbs
or with curry, plain or toasted—
can be taken out and happily come
in mini sizes. There is a range
of hot dishes too like quiches and
vegetable crumble and the delicious
deserts include stewed fruits like
rhubarb and strawberry, carrot or
cherry cake, crumbles, tarts, and,
miniature Portuguese pasteis de nata
custard tarts. There are fruit and
vegetable juices of every possible
sort, and a selection of newspapers
and magazines helps one pass
the time.*

LA CRÈMERIE
9, rue des Quatre Vents, 75006
Tel: +33 (0)1 43 54 99 30
(See photographs pp. 75, 146–149)
*An outstanding choice of Italian cold
cuts is offered alongside a selection
of organic, untreated wines.*

DÉLICABAR
Le Bon Marché
26–38, rue de Sèvres, 75007
Tel: +33 (0)1 42 22 10 19
(See photographs pp. 154–157)
*"Light and smooth" are the
watchwords at this eatery on the
first floor of the Grande Épicerie
du Bon Marché located in the middle
of the women's department. Fruit
and vegetable "bubbles," mixed
salads, and mini-sandwiches are
perfect for those worried about
their figure.*

LA FERME
55, rue Saint-Roch, 75001

Tel: +33 (0)1 40 20 12 12
*A rustic chalet style interior for this
specialist in organic foods to eat
in or take out. Discover the Portuguese
pasteis de nata and ice creams from
Martine Lambert in Deauville.*

HANDMADE
19, rue Jean Mermoz, 75008
Tel: +33 (0)1 45 62 50 05
> Other address:
  BHV Café, 11, rue des Archives,
  75004
  Tel: +33 (0)1 49 96 38 91)
*More than a café—this is a bookshop,
fine food store, and a florist.*

LINA'S
13, rue Médicis, 75006
Tel: +33 (0)1 43 25 55 55
Fax: +33 (0)1 43 29 14 14
> Other address:
  50, rue Etienne-Marcel, 75002
*A chain of upmarket sandwich
shops that also has soups, salads,
and deserts for eating in or taking
out. An "American" atmosphere reigns
here, so no need to feel guilty as you
linger over one of the newspapers
available while having lunch.*

POMZE
109, boulevard Haussmann, 75009
Tel: +33 (0)1 42 65 65 83
www.pomze.com
E-mail: contact@pomze.com
(See photographs pp. 158–160)
*Freshly pressed apple juice, cider, and
calvados are available at this boutique
devoted to everything to do with
apples. On the first floor, a very
pleasant restaurant has a choice of
dishes, all of which include apples
in one form or another.*

Pierre Rival wishes to thank Pierre Léonforté for his
friendship, Ghislaine Bavoillot for her attention to every
last gourmet detail, and the whole team at Flammarion for
their stoic patience.

The editors wish to thank all the shop owners who so kindly
opened their doors and allowed us to take the photographs
in this book. They would also like to thank Jean Tiffon and
Diane Gaudin for their help with this book.

Translated from the French by Sheila O'Leary
Copyediting: Chrisoula Petridis
Typesetting: Thierry Renard
Proofreading: Slade Smith
Color separation: Penez Éditions

Distributed in North America by Rizzoli International
Publications, Inc.

Previously published in French as *Paris Gourmand:
Belles et bonnes boutiques de la ville*
© Éditions Flammarion, 2004
English-language edition
© Éditions Flammarion, 2005

www.editions.flammarion.com

05 06 07 4 3 2 1

FC0472-05-II
ISBN: 2-0803-0472-0
Dépôt légal: 02/2005

Printed in Italy by Errestampa